D1715387

A Soldier's Friend,
Civil War Nurse Cornelia Hancock

by Georgiann Baldino

A Pearl Editions, LLC Production

P.O. Box 4197

Naperville, IL 60567-4197

Compilation, notes, chronology and photographs Copyright © 2010
Georgiann Baldino

Published in the United States

Copyright 2010

ISBN   978-0-9828093-0-3

1. Nurses—United States—Biography. 2. Hancock, Cornelia 3.
United States—History—Civil War. 4. Social Reformers—United
States—Biography.

Table of Contents

Civil War Nurse Cornelia Hancock

"Anyone who wants to test his or her or the nation's mettle in a presumed rite of passage—war—should show care and wisdom. It must always be remembered…war was a human ordeal and not an abstract heroic adventure." Al Santoli, *Everything We Had*

Introduction

Cornelia Hancock did not meet the government's requirements for female nurses—and yet she served on the frontlines for nearly two years. Though 150 years have passed, personal stories of the Civil War continue to fascinate, and Cornelia provided a unique look behind the scenes. This book is based on the letters she wrote during and after the Civil War.

However, from Cornelia's letters alone, it is hard to place her against the huge background of the Civil War. She was writing to people who understood the circumstances. To appreciate the momentous events she witnessed, it's necessary to add more detail than she provided.

One example is a letter dated May 30, 1864, in which she wrote: "This morning this place is to be evacuated and the White House is to be the next base. Oh! what a sight. This place was one mass of tired, swearing soldiery, scrambling for a hard tack, killing chickens, pigs, calves, etc. Seems like Bedlam let loose. I am always cared for tho'; before we had been in the town half an hour a guard was detailed over the house, so we slept in perfect security."[1] This passage described Port Royal, Virginia, the location of a Union depot. The next base she referred to was White House Landing in Virginia, not the White House in Washington, D.C. Union commanders had ordered a hasty change of plans. General Ulysses S. Grant disengaged his forces and proceeded southward. Union and Confederate armies raced to the North Anna River and then clashed at the ghastly Second Battle of Cold Harbor, which became a symbol of wanton, wholesale death and destruction—for little gain. The losses were noteworthy even in a war that set unbelievable benchmarks for savagery.[2] Cornelia's presence near this and other earth-shaking battles is hard to believe and hard to understand from the passages she wrote. Putting her experiences into context gave them the treatment they deserve.

If Cornelia had not proven her ability from her first days of service and continually thereafter, she would have been sent home. She succeeded where many other women did not. Once surgeons saw how Cornelia worked, they asked her to serve in their wards, and soldiers relied on her care. "The boys say they will hollar 'Miss Hancock' as soon as they fall."[3] Commanders allowed her to stay because she put soldiers first and did not complain about insults or privation. It took an unshakable sense of duty to get along in a hostile, male environment. When battlefield conditions spiraled out of control, military commanders ordered civilians to leave. Even then, Cornelia found ways to remain on duty.

Working class women did not write narratives about the Civil War. Relatively few written records exist from them, and few historians include women hospital workers in their manuscripts.[4] Accounts from some women tout their success over indifferent surgeons and administrators. Cornelia's accounts were evenhanded. She criticized surgeons, military officers, the government and other women, whenever she found them inept. She praised those who showed dedication—denigrated others for incompetence or drunkenness. Many history books explain the Civil War's grand campaigns. Cornelia gave a human account. In the process she shed light on ways society suppressed women's intelligence and assertiveness. She also showed how an ingenious woman overcame restrictions. Cornelia Hancock's adventures would make an amazing legend—except in her case the heart-rending ordeals were true.

Lifeline for Cornelia Hancock

Born **February 8, 1840**, Hancock's Bridge in Southern New Jersey.

Service as a volunteer nurse:

- **July 6 through August 6, 1863**, Gettysburg, Pennsylvania, field hospital
- **August 6 to early September 1863**, Camp Letterman Gettysburg General Hospital
- **November 19, 1863**, witnessed the dedication of Gettysburg Cemetery
- **October 26, 1863 – February 8, 1864**, Washington, D.C. at Georgetown Heights home for orphaned slave children and hospital for former slaves.
- **February 11 – March 9, 1864**, Brandy Station, Virginia, 3rd Division hospital, 2nd Corps, Winter Camp.
- **May 11, 1864**, return to hospital duty at Belle Plain and Fredericksburg, Virginia.
- **May 28, 1864**, forced march to White House Station, Virginia.
- **June 3 – 19, 1864**, served at White House Station, Virginia.
- **June 20, 1864**, hasty bivouac under Rebel fire to City Point, Virginia, where Cornelia served until September 25, 1864.
- **October 17, 1864**, returned to City Point, remaining at the depot hospital until May 13, 1865.
- **May 23 and 24, 1865,** review of the parade of the Grand Army of the Republic in Washington, D.C.

June 1865 – January 1866, Philadelphia, Pennsylvania, Quakers of Race Street, a center for liberals and philanthropists.
January 1866–1875, Mt. Pleasant, South Carolina, Laing School
1878 Philadelphia, Pennsylvania, The Society for Organizing Charity.
1884–1914, social worker at Wrightsville project in Philadelphia.
1926 died at the age of 87.

"War" by Clara Barton

Women, men said, *would just be in the way.*
They didn't know the difference between work and play.
What did women know of war anyway?
What could they do? Of what use could they be?
They would just scream at the sight of a gun, don't you see.
Imagine their skirts among artillery wheels,
and watch for their flutter as they flee across the fields.
They would faint at the first drop of blood in their sight....
They might pick some lint, and tear up some sheets,
and make us some jellies, and send on their sweets,
and knit some soft socks for Uncle Sam's shoes,
and write us some letters, and tell us the news.
And so it was settled, by common consent,
that husbands or brothers or whoever went,
that the place for the women was in their own homes,
there to patiently wait until victory comes.

Clara Barton worked tirelessly to gain the trust of government officials. She gathered supplies from all over the country and became known as the "Angel of the Battlefield." She cared for wounded men at sixteen different battles. After the war she became a popular lecturer. The notoriety she gained left a mistaken impression that it was common for women to work near the frontlines. However, most women worked in general hospitals in northern cities or well to the rear. Women like Clara Barton were exceptions.

Another exception was Cornelia Hancock.

Growing up in Hancock's Bridge

Not much is known about Cornelia Hancock's childhood. Details about her home, education and practice of religion are sketchy. Her great grandparents, William and Sarah Hancock, emigrated from England to southern New Jersey in the seventeenth century. William Hancock was one of the investors in the Fenwick Colony. Shortly after the Colony became established in New Salem in 1675, Hancock arrived and received his share of the land, 968 acres in Alloway's Creek, just five miles from Salem. William and Sarah Hancock built their home near the edge of a tidewater marsh.

Later men of the family served as colonial judges and legislators. By the Revolutionary War the family's first home served as a Quaker meeting house and tavern. A small militia gathered there to prevent the British from crossing John Hancock's Bridge, one of three bridges that crossed Alloway's Creek, a tributary of the Delaware River. British Redcoats burst simultaneously from the front and back into the tavern and bayoneted all occupants, including Cornelia's great-grandfather, without regard to whether they were part of the rebel militia or loyal to Britain. The attack and martyrdom added to the family's reputation for their part in developing the new nation.

Cornelia was born February 8, 1840, in Hancock's Bridge, New Jersey. She was the fourth of five children, and the youngest daughter of Thomas Y. and Rachel Hancock. She was a Quaker, literate and middle-class.

She described her father as a silent man, who spent his time thinking, reading the newspapers and fishing in Alloway's Creek. His reputation for silence bordered on eccentricity. Though Thomas Hancock had inherited enough money and property for an education, he had no desire to go to college. Cornelia never knew her father to have any occupation.[5] He worked on the farm only as long as necessary to provide meals for the family. He went to bed with the tide and got up when it turned, planning his days around slack water and fishing. Thomas took six of the best fish for the family table and gave away the rest to village people. Because they had sufficient means to live on, it never occurred to him to sell the bounty to add to the family income.

Tidewater Marsh in Hancock's Bridge, as it appeared in 2009

Cornelia wrote that she and her brother Will had to thank her maternal grandmother for providing the ambition to overcome their father's inertia. Growing up she never lacked the necessities of life, but Cornelia had to rely on help and financial assistance from her cousins Sarah Hancock Gibbon and Henrietta Hancock to receive a good education.[6] When grown, Cornelia had honey-colored hair and little curls, escaping from the smooth knot at the back of her head; dark blue eyes; and stood scarcely five feet tall.[7]

The religious instruction she had growing up was that belief shows itself in daily living—religion was a way of life, not just a set of doctrines. Piety was reflected in every facet of living.

Their worship consisted of enlightened meditation. Cornelia's biographer, Jane T. McConnell indicated as a child Cornelia learned an individual's highest obligation was to follow her conscience. The Society of Friends called their meditation "centering down." Their saying was, "Do the duty that lies nearest thee, wisely improve the present; it is thine."[8] But Cornelia was too energetic for the quiet, rural community and longed to escape Hancock's Bridge.[9]

Cornelia had been brought up to be nonviolent. Quakers had a long tradition of opposing war. The moral dilemma she faced was similar to that of Secretary of War, Edwin Stanton, who was also a Quaker. As a young man, Stanton wondered why "military leaders should be praised instead of treated as malefactors." The outrage of slavery decided the issue for Cornelia. Though she hated war, she was even more opposed to bondage and oppression. Cornelia's conscience told her she must participate in the struggle for slaves' freedom.[10]

When Civil War soldiers came home to recover from injuries, the men told stories of hardship. Critics of army surgeons called medical care at the front "butchery."[11] Newspapers published soldiers' letters that described the failure of medical staff to combat epidemics or care for wounded men. Lists of killed, missing and wounded men filled page after page of newsprint. Cornelia's brother, Will, her male friends and cousins went off to fight. Anxiety for their safety made her frantic to follow.

Cornelia confided her determination to volunteer to her brother-in-law Dr. Henry T. Child, a physician and philanthropist from Philadelphia. He promised to send for her at the first opportunity. When he heard news of a battle being fought in Pennsylvania, Dr. Child sent a carriage before dawn on the morning of July 5, 1863. Cornelia was just 23 years old, and the prospect of her youngest daughter riding away must have been painful for Rachel Hancock. Her youngest son, Thomas, had drowned years before in the creek bordering the farm, and William, the only living son, had already gone off to war. Mrs. Hancock questioned Cornelia, who replied she had made her decision with the aid of the "inner light."[12] Those answers settled the matter between mother and daughter. Her parents had long ago granted Cornelia the right to decide her own line of duty.

She had packed her belongings weeks ago. Within an hour she was off. When the carriage passed through town, Cornelia's friends were on their way to church. She crouched out of sight, so no one could stop her—or remind her of all the reasons she should not go.

Women as Army Nurses

After all the great Civil War battles, women showed up to care for wounded soldiers—but they were not well received. Ladies went to the York Peninsula after Union General McClellan's campaign of 1862, but officials soon ordered them to leave. Throughout the war, women tried to give lifesaving aid to wounded and ill soldiers—but faced stiff opposition from military officials. The army allowed regiments to use laundresses at camp. Female sutlers or vivandières[a] peddled goods to soldiers, but during campaigns soldiers were on their own.[13] The vast majority of women who served worked in general hospitals in the North or well to the rear. The number who helped at the front was never large; the women who followed the troops were rarest of all.

Many women fancied themselves capable of enduring the rigors of hospital life, but any woman who kept her place in a general or corps hospital had to prove trustworthiness, tact, discretion, endurance and strength of nerve. No woman gave continual hospital service who was not an exceptional person with compassion, a clear head, enthusiasm, courage, and firmness—one in a thousand.[14] Many of the women who went lasted little more than a month. The physical and emotional challenges wore them down—or illness made it impossible to continue. Louisa May Alcott is one example of a woman who worked at Union Hospital in Washington, D.C. but fell desperately ill with typhoid after only six weeks. Hannah Ropes also contracted typhoid fever in 1862 while serving in the same hospital. Ropes died in January 1863. Louisa May Alcott eventually recovered, but the treatment, which included mercury, affected her health for the rest of her life. The total number of nurses who died from typhoid fever and other causes is not known.[15]

---

[a] A woman who brought provisions and liquor to troops in the field, as in the French Army.

Like veteran troops, successful women nurses became battle-hardened. Their enemies were disease, infection, and a system that too often ignored the soldiers' humanity.[16] Their duties were to dress wounds, change linens, assist during surgery, pass out medications and prepare meals. They also did unthinkable things such as walking away from dying men they could not help. Cornelia and the others knew that it was heartless to let men die unattended, but scores of others waited. They forced themselves to move on to someone with the hope of survival.

To remain on duty women nurses had to work within a flawed system. Wherever Cornelia served, she had no official standing. She was a volunteer, received no pay, got scant allowances, and was free to leave at any time—and the reasons to go home were overwhelming. Despite this, Cornelia remained determined to serve near the fighting. She is less well known than Clara Barton, but similar to Barton in that, despite Army restrictions, both women made their way to the frontlines.

Wherever they served, volunteer nurses experienced first-hand the grim realities of war—amputated limbs, mutilated bodies, disease and death. They provided invaluable aid to the sick and wounded soldiers on both sides. Dorothea Dix led a national effort to organize a nursing corps. She had visited East Cambridge Jail in 1841 to teach a Sunday school class for women inmates. She found prostitutes, drunks, criminals, retarded individuals, and the mentally ill all housed together in unheated, unfurnished, and foul-smelling quarters. Dix visited other jails and almshouses in Boston and soon her investigations extended over the entire state of Massachusetts, wherever mentally ill were housed. She collected data and shaped it into a carefully worded document, which was delivered to the Massachusetts legislature. The material won legislative support and funds were set aside for the expansion of Worcester State Hospital. From there, Dix played a major role in improving treatment for the insane in the United States.[17] She also had gone to Britain, Turkey and the Crimea to work with Florence Nightingale.

In May 1861 Surgeon General R. C. Wood appointed Dix to organize a nursing corps of female volunteers and recruit women.

Within a year she was battling with army doctors.[18] Military traditionalists opposed her, but her indomitable will and a singleness of purpose kept her going. "In those days it was considered indecorous for angels of mercy to appear otherwise than gray-haired and spectacled...a hospital corps of comely young maiden nurses, possessing grace and good looks, was then unknown."[19] Recruits nicknamed her "Dragon Dix." The epithet was a reflection of what it took to succeed in creating the military's first professional nursing corps, but her confrontational style worked against her and male acceptance of women nurses.

Women who volunteered to work under the Dix administration had to meet strict guidelines. Consequently women looked for other ways to serve.[20] Many of the women who worked independently served without pay. Records for these women were lost or poorly kept. One significant example of unpaid work was the service of Catholic nuns, who helped both North and South. Southern women also nursed soldiers without pay at home or in churches because the war came to them. In both cases their work was never recorded or compensated.[21] In Cornelia's letters she mentioned that she should be entitled to a salary of $12 per month but only received $9.25 for nearly two years of work.

Of the women who worked independently, Clara Barton is the most well-known.[22] She recognized the first thing women needed to do was overcome attitudes they harbored about themselves: "I struggled long and hard with my sense of propriety," Barton said, "with the appalling fact that I was a woman, whispering in one ear, and groans of suffering men, dying like dogs, unfed and unsheltered, for the life of the very institutions which had protected and educated me, thundering in the other. I said that I struggled with my sense of propriety, and I say it with shame before God and before you, I am ashamed that I thought of such a thing."[23]

Cornelia also faced the scandal caused by any young woman, who lived near the front. "Sarah S_ wrote me a letter expressive of great concern from my 'way of living.' I wrote her a letter that she will not soon forget. They cannot expect everyone to be satisfied to live in as small a circle as themselves in these days of great events.

She expresses it as the great concern of the whole family."[24] A number of times people with suspect motives spread gossip about Cornelia. She attributed the rumors to jealousy and her "off hand manner."[25] Then she goes on to assure her family that they can rely on her to do her "straightforward duty."

Neighbors back home in Salem, New Jersey, felt Cornelia needed to have another woman with her as a chaperone. In response Cornelia wrote, "I am much better guarded than lone widows" [at home,] that another woman was not needed and would not be allowed.[26] Cornelia confirmed that, as long as she held herself out as a lady, soldiers treated her with respect. One example she gave was a letter from an unnamed, wounded soldier, who had been evacuated to Baltimore. "Please excuse a Soldier for taking the liberty to write to you, for although we are Soldiers we know how to appreciate a kind act. Your sincere friend, A Soldier."[27]

Army surgeons, who wanted to keep women out of the hospitals, more readily accepted Catholic nuns. They praised nuns for being more faithful and devoted. The Sisters also had nursing experience because Catholic orders maintained hospitals for society's poor. Twelve orders of nuns volunteered in the Civil War, including several branches of Sisters of Charity, Sisters of Mercy, Sisters of St. Joseph and Sisters of the Holy Cross.[28] Many lay nurses did not equal the efficiency and faithfulness of Catholic Sisters.[29]

Privately Cornelia evaluated the Army's nursing corps this way: "Miss Dix's nurses are like all others in my estimation: some excellent, some good, some positively bad."[30] She noted that, for some females, the hospital represented a "capital place to get a husband. Many good-looking women gallivanted around in evening and had a good time," but Cornelia did not volunteer for that reason and never troubled herself with the "common herd."[31]

Initiation at Gettysburg

Late in the day, July 5, 1863, Cornelia's carriage reached Philadelphia. The city had gone wild with news of a terrible battle fought on Pennsylvania soil—no one knew exactly where—but "it finally became known to be a town called Gettysburg."[32] Dr. Child wanted to leave that evening on the 11 p.m. train. He helped Miss Eliza Farnham and a number of other women of "suitable age" get passes as volunteer nurses. These ladies were many years older than Cornelia, and Dr. Child selected Miss Farnham to watch over her.

The next morning the train arrived in Baltimore, where Superintendent Dorthea Dix appeared on the scene. Her regulations decreed no women candidates under 30 years of age would be accepted for service. Candidates must be matronly women with strong health and the capacity to care for the sick. They must wear plain dress, brown, gray or black, and no hoop skirts. Unlike most women at the time, Cornelia did not wear hoop skirts, but that apparently was not a deciding factor.

Miss Dix looked over the candidates and pronounced them acceptable—except Cornelia. Dix took one look and rejected her as being too young and rosy cheeked. Miss Farnham tried to argue with Miss Dix, and the discussion "waxed warm." Cornelia didn't wait to see what they decided. She settled the question for herself and returned to the train, vowing they would have to remove her forcibly. A conductor helped her hide in a baggage car and told no one, except Dr. Child, where Cornelia had gone. When she arrived at Gettysburg, the crushing needs silenced any concerns about her age or complexion.[33]

Enlisted men filled many more Civil War nursing positions than women. Commanders detailed soldiers to care for the sick and wounded, but combat officers hated to assign men who would be useful in battle. Instead they filled nursing positions with misfits, malingers, those skilled at finding soft jobs behind the frontlines—or men recovering from their own injuries.[34] The only soldier with lower rank than a private was a sick private because he used up valuable resources. Sick soldiers ranked near the bottom of the military hierarchy—but above women who had the lowest status of all. Women had little influence with surgeons or hospital stewards. If they tried to lobby for more humane care, most of the time female nurses were unsuccessful.[35]

All nurses, male and female, lacked training and had to be taught what to do in the field. As a group, disabled or undisciplined soldiers made the worst caregivers. Surgeon Alfred L. Castleman wrote how difficult it was to use men who were unskilled and in poor health. "This morning," he wrote, "as my newly appointed nurses came in, I was utterly disheartened. There is not a man amongst them who can make a toast...yet the sick must depend on them for all their cooking. Half of them are applicants for discharge on the ground of disability, yet they are sent to me to work over the sick....Not one has ever dispensed a dose of medicine....I do the best I can [for our sick and wounded] but when I have trained men...it is hard they should now be taken from me, at the very moment of expected battle, and replaced with such as these."[36] By the time a soldier learned the nurse's job and began to do it well, he often was ordered back to active duty.[37]

Mary Livermore, who directed the Northwestern branch of the Sanitary Commission, described the way women felt about their husbands, sons and lovers at the front. "Especially did women refuse to release their hold on the men of their households. They followed them with tender anxiety and intelligent provision."[38] However, they did not follow their men folk in person. Instead most women collected and sent stores of goods.

To ease her anxiety about family members and friends, Cornelia wanted to be on the scene. She defended her choice to leave home this way: "There was no impropriety for a young person to be there, provided they were sensible. All the soldiers were most polite and obliging.[39] The Salem people's concern has no effect upon me whatever. You cannot know how we live here unless you could be here. There is no danger from anything in the army except an unsophisticated individual might have [her] affections trifled."[40]

Still, society rejected the idea women could live and work near military camps. It was deemed improper for women to care for men outside of their immediate families. Even though the government regulations required medical officers to engage women, many refused to allow women in their hospitals. Elite officers, who observed the rules of polite society at home, spoke and acted rougher than privates and had no qualms about verbally abusing nurses. If upper class women volunteered, no one deferred to them any longer.[41] They had to learn how to get on without any preferential treatment. Cornelia was no exception. Once established at the front, she lamented, "The Salem people[b] do not write to me at all now…they have given me over for a reprobate entirely."[42] Newspaper articles that praised her contribution made no difference to some of her neighbors. In fact, publicity made things worse. "A piece in the paper made a great stir."[43]

In sharp contrast to what stay-at-home society believed, women like Cornelia had a calming influence on the soldiers. Women became peacemakers. They reminded soldiers about civility, home and hearth. Still—on both sides, North and South—women worried more about people at home who doubted their morals than they did about sexual predators.[44] Rowdy veterans became respectful and even docile in the presence of a woman. Wounded men on both sides preferred female to male caregivers.[45] Experts estimate only one man out of 10 had ever been completely without the care of a mother, sister or wife.[46] Cornelia put the men's longing for reminders of home into perspective and stressed how grateful men were to see a woman at the front. "The whole Potomac Army stretches from Alexandria to Culpepper….there have been many over from the Regiments round; their sole purpose seeming to be to see a lady. After they take a good look they start back seemingly contented."[47]

At times, it was difficult for the wounded soldiers to express how much it helped to have a woman caregiver. Sophronia Bucklin, one of Dorthea Dix's nurses, recorded an incident that illustrated this. "One poor fellow, whose eyes were both shot out, with his head badly shattered, lay silent while his ablutions were being performed. I thought he had perhaps lost his speech in the untold terror it was….I could not comb his hair, for the bandages were bound tightly over

---

[b] Salem County, New Jersey.

it…he turned away….I passed on without questioning him. A few days went by, then he said, 'Did you notice that I never talked to you as other patients did, when you first came to take care of us?…I will tell you why,' he continued; 'I was so thankful, that I had no words for speech—to think the women of the North should come down here, and do so much for us, being exposed to all kinds of disease, and to do so much work and hard fare, all to take care of us poor soldiers, when we lie as I do.'"[48] Cornelia's papers include letters she received from ambulance drivers and enlisted men. "You will never be forgotten by us for we often think of your kind acts and remember them with pleasure."[49] Whether approved by Dix or not, Cornelia was determined to serve near battlefields. She started out writing letters for desperately wounded men and quickly moved on to making meals, dressing wounds, administering medicine, assisting in surgery, whatever needed to be done.

A Nation Unprepared

At the opening of the war, the surgeon-general of the regular army was 80-year-old Thomas Lawson, a veteran of the War of 1812 and Mexican War. His major concern was keeping costs down. His replacement, Alexander Finlay, also worried about the budget. He waited for a battle before ordering supplies.[50] The rest of the staff consisted of 30 surgeons with the rank of major, and 84 assistant surgeons with the rank of first lieutenant for the first five years of service. There was no hospital corps; the necessary nursing and other hospital assistance was performed by soldiers temporarily detailed to hospital duty.

The country had only 115 trained medical officers at the beginning of the war, and these paltry numbers were quickly depleted. Twenty-seven doctors resigned their Union positions. Three went into private practice because they refused to assist either the North or South. Twenty-four transferred to the Confederacy, where they received powerful positions.[51]

Another group with the designation of Acting Assistant Surgeons were private physicians, uncommissioned, serving under contract in field or in general hospitals. This class had some of the most eminent surgeons and physicians of the country. Medical Cadets were generally young medical students assigned to general hospitals as dressers and assistants. The Medical Department also enlisted Hospital Stewards as needed to perform the duties of druggists, clerks, and storekeepers.[52]

In 1861 the only military hospital in Washington was a six-room building, used for smallpox patients.[53] Public hospitals were insignificant places, used to house the working poor and discarded members of society. Hospitals served the indigent and were places of squalor. No examples of the kind of facilities the country needed existed. Good hospitals would have to be developed.[54] Meanwhile, a flood of sick and wounded overwhelmed the military.

During the early battles like the 1861 Battle of Bull Run, the Union was not even prepared to bring the wounded off the battlefield. Independent ambulance service, like hospitals, had to be built. Commanders further compromised battlefield aid because they failed to guard the field hospitals.

Division hospital personnel consisted of: a surgeon in charge, an assistant surgeon as executive officer, a second assistant surgeon as recorder, operating staff of three surgeons aided by three assistant surgeons, nurses and attendants. Army regulations allowed one nurse for every 10 beds. By the end of the war, the single, six-room hospital had been replaced by a vast medical system with 400,000 beds to care for soldiers.[55]

Medical officers accompanied their regiments and established temporary dressing stations as near as they could to the line of battle. Regulations stated: "Ravines and woods should be taken advantage of as a protection against the enemy's fire; if necessary, a breastwork[c] can be thrown up by the attendants. An occasional bullet or an occasional shell is not sufficient to warrant Medical Officers in leaving their posts." However, regulations could not begin to cover the confusion of shifting lines during major battles. At Gettysburg, for example, a tremendous artillery duel along Seminary Ridge transformed a "sunny day into a fog of gunpowder."[56]

---

[c] A defensive wall hastily constructed often protecting the summit of a mound.

When armies moved into the field, medical staffs had huge problems transporting vital equipment. Generally speaking, ammunition went forward first, rations second—medical supplies third. Because of the tremendous number of men involved, roads clogged. When large armies confronted each other, nothing but bare necessities got to the front. Medical personnel suffered along with the troops. "On the march," Cornelia wrote, "we were reduced to hardtack and uncooked pork, and I actually ate it with keen relish."[57]

The regiment was the most important unit for infantrymen. Soldiers wanted to serve and die with their friends. Small regiments were the way the military delivered medical treatment.[d] Lincoln directed state governors to appoint a surgeon and assistant surgeon for each volunteer regiment. To a large degree hometown doctors lacked the training necessary to prepare them for the way large-caliber bullets splintered and crushed bones. Yet soldiers only trusted physicians from back home.

During the chaos of battle, the regiment-only approach to administering care broke down and cost countless lives. Regimental hospitals, when overwhelmed trying to care for their wounded, turned away wounded from other regiments.[58] Disorder and frustration ruled. In 1861 none of the artillery batteries or cavalry detachments had their own medical officers.[59] At first, regimental band members carried the wounded off the field, but soon there were no band members left.

In early battles, many of the ambulance drivers were civilians. Drivers feared for their safety, got drunk on medicinal liquor and ignored the wounded while they hid from enemy fire.[60] Witnesses reported that a one-eyed man in the Ambulance Corps neglected wounded soldiers so he could rob corpses.[61] A man's friend might leave the fight to carry him off the field, but this seriously depleted the infantry. When soldiers couldn't find the proper field hospital, they rarely returned to action.[62] A number of men assigned to work as

---

[d] The official size of a regiment was 1,000 men. Four or five infantry regiments of 1,000 men made up a brigade; three or four brigades made up a division of up to 15,000 soldiers; and three divisions made up a Corps. See Appendix I for more details about how fighting units were organized.

regimental litter bearers showed cowardice. It required more guards to watch them and see that they did their duty than their services were worth.[63]

At the outset of the war, the Medical Department and quartermasters split responsibility for ambulance service. As long as this was the case, the drivers would not take orders from doctors.[64] The ambulance wagons and carts often broke down or disappeared because quartermasters used them to transport officers and munitions instead of take care of fallen soldiers. As a result, many of the wounded had to find the field hospitals under their own power.

In August 1862 General George McClellan created the Ambulance Corps for the Army of the Potomac under the control of the Medical Director. The Quartermaster Corps, which wanted to retain control of ambulances and drivers, and some field commanders loudly opposed McClelland's order to reorganize, but removing ambulances from the quartermasters vastly improved the evacuation of the wounded from the battlefield. Despite the success in the east, Congress did not create an Ambulance Corps for all the Union Armies until March 1864.[65] Cornelia witnessed many overwhelming sights, but to her the most melancholy one was seeing long trains of ambulances come in after night fall.[66]

Cornelia also documented the stress placed on wounded men. June 3, 1864, she wrote: "I arrived at this place yesterday having joined a train of wounded coming from the battlefield with Dr. Aiken. We got opposite the White House [Virginia] and found no bridge and were obliged to keep our wounded in the ambulances 12 hours longer making two days & nights they had been loaded and on the way....you can hardly imagine the appearance of our wounded now brought from the field after having been under fire for 21 precarious days. They hardly look like men."[67]

While units were on the move, it was impossible to wash. An army on the march could be smelled before it was seen.[68] Cornelia gave a sympathetic example, "I took water from the [James] River and washed the face and hands of all wounded in our Div. train; no one can know the relief one feels in using water after a three day's march." She further described the rigors of forced marches. "The soldiers dread the summer's campaign but always speak with more feeling of the march than the fighting."[69] On days that grew very hot, the troops suffered from lack of drinking water. Men became sunstruck. Soldiers on forced marches dropped out of their ranks from exhaustion.[70]

The lack of basic services and poor quality of care makes it hard to imagine how soldiers maintained stamina to fight or the will to go on. Cornelia uses straightforward language to describe how these deficiencies affected soldiers. "The drums beat, the bugle sounds, the winds blow, the men groan."[71]

The wounded were supposed to be removed from the battlefield on hand litters,[72] but many other means were used. Stout sticks or muskets were passed through the sleeves of a coat, or rolled into the edges of blankets to make a litter. Hurdles, gates, or ladders with blankets or straw thrown over them made useful stretchers. Poles interlaced with ropes or telegraph wire were also fashioned into litters. Soldiers, waiting for evacuation, endured lingering agony. Many of these men showed greater courage than those who died immediately. Other wounded soldiers walked out on their own. Jonathan Letterman, Medical Director for the Army of the Potomac, not only convinced General George McClellan to form an Ambulance Corps under medical control, but also to train stretcher bearers.[73] General McClelland adopted Letterman's recommendations in 1862, and General Grant followed with a similar order for his western units in March of 1863. Throughout the remainder of the war, drivers parked ambulances together to deter officers from using them for non-medical reasons.[74]

By September 1862 officials in Washington were only beginning to make necessary changes. That month at Antietam, the new ambulance system started to work, but quartermasters still delayed delivery of medical supplies. The Sanitary Commission and other private relief agencies filled the gap. They raised money for supplies; bought, borrowed or hired wagons; and sent them through—often ahead of the military.[75] In January 1863 reforms became federal law and outdated regulations were replaced. Even so, wounded boys continued to languish for hours after a battle, pleading for medical assistance. Sanitary Commission agents spied on the Army of the Potomac and determined where the next battle would occur, so they could establish supply depots nearby. Sanitary Commission foresight proved invaluable at Gettysburg.[76] Cornelia indicated on July 8, 1863, four days after the battle ended, "The Christian Committee support us and when they get tired the Sanitary is on hand. Uncle Sam is very rich, but very slow, and if it were not for the Sanitary, much suffering would ensue."[77]

Compared to modern military expenditures, appropriations from Congress were miserly. Top ranking medical and administrative personnel attained their positions solely based on seniority. Peacetime regulations left the government unprepared to cope with the emergencies of all-out war, and improvements were slow in coming. State governors appointed surgeons and assistants based on political influence, not skill or professional knowledge. Reports tell of surgeons who had no idea where to amputate a man's arm or how to suture blood vessels. The lack of skill extended to administrative duties; too many surgeons didn't know what items the purveyors stocked or how to requisition supplies.

The medicine chest, mess chest, and bulky hospital supplies were transported in wagons of the field train and were usually far in the rear—and inaccessible when needed most. The medical and surgical equipment available on the firing line was what the surgeon carried in his case, known as the "surgeon's field companion," and what his orderly brought in the "hospital knapsack," a bulky affair weighing about 20 pounds. When full, it contained opium, paregoric, ipecac, brandy, quinine, tourniquets, bandages, lint, sponges and candles.[78]

Despite strong opposition from the military, the United States Sanitary Commission, the leading prelate[e] relief organization of the Civil War period, was created in June 1861. Reverend Henry W. Bellows was President; the famous landscape architect, Frederick Law Olmsted, was Secretary; and the Commission enlisted scores of physicians and literally hundreds of public-spirited men and women.

---

[e] In addition to supplies and medical care the Commission wanted to improve morality among soldiers and passed out religious tracts, books and Bibles.

Their first year of operation a Sanitary Commission report rated 200 surgeons as follows: 129 competent, 25 tolerable, 19 negligent or inert.[79] A hospital inspection report that year covered 200 facilities and rated 105 as good, 52 as tolerable, and 26 as bad, stating supplies were poor, the diet limited, and nursing care terrible with no nurses on duty at night.[80]

Mary A. Livermore, associate member of the Sanitary Commission, indicates that the object of the Sanitary Commission was to do what government could not: The Government undertook, of course, to provide all that was necessary for the soldier,…but, from the very nature of things, this was not possible…The methods of the commission were so elastic, and so arranged to meet every emergency, that it was able to make provision for any need, seeking always to supplement, and never to supplant, the Government. The Sanitary Commission collected and forwarded boxes of food to soldiers, provided clothing, private aid to soldiers and to their dependents, took care of fugitives, and helped out with nursing and hospital care.

The Sanitary Commission also hired or enlisted volunteer inspectors and provided them with detailed guidelines on the best ways to conduct investigations. Inspectors asked for the approval of the superior officers before they entered a camp, and permission was usually given. They assessed the location of the camp, drainage, ventilation of tents or quarters, the quality of the rations, the methods of cooking, general cleanliness of the camp and the men. They reviewed diet and cooking. Wherever they found unhealthy conditions, they pointed out the problems tactfully to the commanders and sent reports to the commission. These reports contained immense amounts of information, which their actuaries tabulated and physicians reviewed. The effects were usually good. Commanders, when made aware of problems, were less likely to repeat mistakes in the future. Regiments with good sanitary and hygienic conditions provided examples for other units. Eminent medical men used the information gathered to prepare 18 short treatises, which were distributed to regimental surgeons and commanding officers. Military surgeons valued these books highly.

Members of the commission included some of the best-known physicians in the country. Influential members were successful in influencing public opinion, which resulted in passage of a bill that, to a large extent, removed the system of promoting military surgeons based on seniority. In terms of direct aid to Union soldiers, the Sanitary Commission raised almost five million dollars as well as supplies valued at $15 million to improve conditions for Union soldiers.[81] The U.S. Christian Commission collected an additional $3.5 million in aid. [82] At the time of the Peninsular campaign, March through July 1862, the Commission obtained hospital transports for the wounded.[83] As fighting dragged on, the Sanitary Commission continued to provide inspections, medical transport, hygiene, sanitation, and construction of hospitals. Even though they were outside of the government, the Commission concerned itself with every facet of war and brought about reforms.[84]

Frederick Law Olmstead, Executive Secretary of the Sanitary Commission, blamed poor morale among Union troops on poor leadership. "When a man who has, through patriotic impulse volunteered to service his country on the field of battle and falls dangerously ill, or has a leg shot off, he cannot feel …[that] proper clothing …nourishing food, surgical attendance depends on the charity of others."[85] Cornelia described the impact private agencies had. "The Sanitary Commission is worth its weight in gold. They certainly have got together a humane and noble set of men to execute its business—and that class of men in Washington is so scarce."[86]

Caring for the wounded presented medical officers with challenges none of them could have imagined at the war's outset. The cleanliness of wounds, except for removing large pieces of debris, was regarded as having little or no importance. Units carried only a few, scanty dressings into action. An injured soldier covered his wounds as best he could with a dirty handkerchief or piece of cloth torn from a sweaty shirt. Elastic bandages for controlling hemorrhage were unknown; the surgeon relied, except in the case of larger vessels, on packing the wound with astringent, coagulant, and generally harmful chemicals.

Most of the medicines they carried were in pill form, but tablets of the era were hard to dissolve and produced unreliable results. They carried medicine as pills because liquids were much more difficult to transport without losing.

Crude drugs, such as opium, were available instead of the refined, active ingredients like morphine that doctors now use. Having opium on the battlefield prevented an enormous amount of suffering. Opiates were one of the few valuable drug treatments available to physicians. It was also used to treat diarrhea. Opium was in widespread use for civilians as well as in the military. It was given to children as young as one month in teething syrup. Army doctors gave opiates out liberally. This led to some problem with addiction.[87] Another problem drug was mercury, which was regularly given for diarrhea, dysentery and typhoid fever—often enough that men died from mercury toxicity.

Doctors applied turpentine on bandages to keep maggots from infesting wounds. They also gave turpentine orally for chronic diarrhea and typhoid fever.[88]

Surgeons didn't have any of the heart stimulants modern medical science uses so effectively. Many of their therapies were ineffective or even harmful, so doctors emphasized diet. Attending physicians wrote diet plans and, in the general and rehabilitation hospitals, special diet kitchens followed what they prescribed.[89]

Physicians of the era could not envision wounds healing without inflammation. Months of rations consisting of salted meats and no fresh vegetables or fruits caused massive outbreaks of scurvy, or Vitamin C deficiency, and left many soldiers weak and lethargic.[90] Long tours of duty with an inadequate diet led to scurvy, night blindness and malnutrition that contributed to the number of fatalities. A comparison between the incidence of scurvy and fatality rates showed that when scurvy was less frequent, wound mortality fell.[91] Even under the best conditions, physicians expected wound repair to be a slow, painful, and exhausting process. This was an era when the presence of pus was considered a positive sign and part of the healing process.[92] One assistant surgeon reported, "It was like the days when there was no king in Israel, and every man did what was right in his own eyes."[93]

One of the more than 100 field hospital locations at Gettysburg

The official record indicates every effort was made to treat wounded men within 48 hours. Most primary care was administered at field hospitals located behind the frontlines. Those who survived were then transported in unreliable and overcrowded ambulances, two-wheeled carts or four-wheeled wagons to army hospitals located in nearby cities and towns.[94] Cornelia puts a human face on the tragedy of those journeys, [Wounded soldiers] "arrived at night when all the ladies would…feed them as they came in. [Men] would then remain in the ambulance until morning when probably no shelter could be procured for them and here they lay in the scorching sun during ½ the day. It was at this time there was such crying need to dress their wounds, some of which had not been opened for 36 hours." In other words, a soldier could wait for hours on the battlefield, endure an excruciating cart ride, only to be dropped at the field hospital and left exposed to the elements. If he survived this treatment and started to recover, a wounded man endured another difficult evacuation to a general hospital. "Two mortal hours we sat in the sun, heard the locomotive hiss, the cars go back and go ahead, then back, just what happens at depots," meanwhile 500 wounded men waited to be evacuated.[95]

Nursing was the most effective part of medical treatment in the nineteenth century. Female nurses proved their worth and made significant contributions—by improving filthy conditions, making care more humane and providing palatable food.

The Battle of Gettysburg

Union and Confederate armies fought at Gettysburg from early morning July 1 to late in the day on July 3, 1863. It was a critical battle for the country and the most costly one of the war, based on the number of casualties.

Up to this point the military advantage in the eastern part of the country had been with the South. Union soldiers' spirits were at a low point, and President Lincoln had just taken command of the Army of the Potomac away from General Joseph Hooker and replaced him with General George G. Meade. His first day in command, just two days before the battle, Meade was "devoted to gaining a knowledge of the strength and condition of the different corps."[96]

In the western part of the country Vicksburg, Mississippi, was about to surrender to General Grant. Once that happened Grant could turn his forces south or east. General Robert E. Lee decided to invade the North, hoping to draw Union troops away from Vicksburg. He marched into Pennsylvania with the goal of taking its capital city, Harrisburg. Neither Meade nor Lee wanted to fight at Gettysburg, but that is where the two armies collided.

Meade issued a general order on June 30th, telling commanders to speak to their men: "The commanding general requests that, previous to the engagement soon expected with the enemy, corps and all other commanding officers will address their troops, explaining to them briefly the immense issues involved in the struggle. The enemy are on our soil; the whole country now looks anxiously to this army to deliver it from the presence of the foe; our failure to do so will leave us no such welcome as the swelling of millions of hearts with pride and joy at our success would give to every soldier of this army. Homes, firesides, and domestic altars are involved. The army has fought well heretofore; it is believed that it will fight more desperately and bravely than ever if it is addressed in fitting terms." His final sentence sent a strong, chilling message: "Corps and other commanders are authorized to order the instant death of any soldier who fails in his duty this hour."[97]

Another order given before the battle foreshadowed intense suffering for the wounded: "The commanding general has received information that the enemy are advancing, probably in strong force, on Gettysburg. It is the intention to hold this army pretty nearly in the position it now occupies until the plans of the enemy shall have been more fully developed....Corps commanders will hold their commands in readiness at a moment's notice, and upon receiving orders to march against the enemy, their trains (ammunition wagons excepted) must be parked in the rear of the place of concentration. Ammunition wagons and ambulances will alone be permitted to accompany the troops. The men must be provided with three days' rations in haversacks, and with sixty rounds of ammunition in the boxes and upon the person."[98] Union regiments raced to join the fighting at Gettysburg, and troops arrived well before the supply trains.[99] The army endured forced marches to battle sites; many units traveled 30 miles a day. Weary surgeons generally marched along with the men. Most personnel arrived after the fighting had started and had no time to make preparations.[100]

However, the new arrangements for the Ambulance Corp worked well. With some notable exceptions,[f] wounded men came off the battlefield each night. The problem was necessary hospital and surgical supplies had been parked well behind the lines. After fighting had ended, a tremendous thunderstorm struck the evening of July 4, 1863, adding to the misery of the wounded.[101]

Cornelia arrived on July 6, the third day after the enormous battle. Her journey from Hancock's Bridge, New Jersey, took a day and a half. She exchanged the beauty of a rural home with towering butternut trees, situated on the edge of a tidewater marsh—for 25 square miles of devastation. On a personal level it was a horrendous initiation. She saw demolished buildings, shattered trees, crushed

---

[f] Some areas like the Wheat Field became no-man's land where wounded men were not evacuated until after fighting ceased.

artillery wagons, broken muskets scattered in every direction, huge numbers of unused cartridges, cannon balls of all kinds, ramrods and bayonets, as well as bits of clothing, belts, gloves and knapsacks. Some horses knelt in death, their necks arched, as if still proud of the riders on their backs. Mutilated bodies of men lay scattered around in all positions.[102]

Townspeople desperately tried to save wounded soldiers. The population of Gettysburg at the time was 2,400. For every citizen in Gettysburg there were 10 wounded men. Cornelia described the scene this way: "The July sun was mercilessly shining, and at every step the air grew heavier and fouler....As we made our way to the little woods in which we were told was the Field Hospital we were seeking, the first sight that met our eyes was a collection of semi-conscious but still living human forms, all of whom had been shot through the head, and were considered hopeless. They were laid there to die and I hoped that they were indeed too near death to have consciousness. Yet many a groan came from them, and their limbs tossed and twitched."[103]

At Gettysburg over 650 medical officers were present for duty, and they worked day and night with little rest. Dr. Letterman reported: "The labor performed by these officers was immense. Some of them fainted from exhaustion. ...Their conduct as officers and as professional men was admirable. Thirteen of them were wounded, one of whom died on July 6th from the effects of his wounds, received on the 3rd. The idea, very prevalent, that medical officers are not exposed to fire, is thus shown to be wholly erroneous."[104] Three days of fighting left 51,000 Union and Confederate men killed, wounded, missing or captured.

When the armies ceased fire, every farm field became a graveyard and every church, public building and even private homes became hospitals.[105] After Pickett's Charge, the desperate Confederate attempt to salvage victory, dead and wounded littered a huge area.

Late in the day on July 4 General Lee started to move the Army of Northern Virginia away from the battle. General Meade's units followed, although not in hot pursuit. The southern army loaded as many of their wounded as they could onto a long, sorrowful wagon train but left behind 5,500 men too severely hurt to survive the journey.[106] General Lee placed John D. Imboden in charge of the supply train and column of wounded. This Confederate caravan retreated through Fairfield, Pennsylvania, where young boys tore out spokes of the wagon wheels with stakes. General Imboden ordered that the next boy to destroy a wagon would be hung. He abandoned the broken wagons and continued to retreat without rest.[107]

The first day Cornelia was in Gettysburg she realized she was too inexperienced to nurse, so she went from man to man with "pencil, paper and stamps. To many mothers, sisters and wives, all night long I penned the last message of those soon to become the 'beloved dead.'"[108] These letters were significant acts of mercy. Most of the time, families did not hear about a soldier's fate. By war's end, hundreds of thousands of men were buried in undocumented locations. The lists of dead and wounded published in newspapers were inaccurate and grossly incomplete. It is estimated that forty percent of Union soldiers and a far greater number of Confederates who died were described as "unknown." Even in military hospitals, casualties were not properly recorded.[109] When Cornelia wrote letters like these for dying men, she provided comfort many loved ones never received.

Before fighting ended at Gettysburg, the supply of doctors and ambulances was described as adequate, but when General Meade pursued the Confederates, the Union took many of the resources with them. Approximately 100 surgeons stayed behind, but they had few supplies. Dr. Jonathan Letterman described the situation in this way: "The time for primary operations had passed, and what remained to be done was to attend to making the men comfortable, dress their wounds, and perform such secondary operations as from time to time might be necessary. One hundred and six medical officers were left behind when the army left; no more could be left, as it was expected that another battle would within three or four days take place."[110]

A few Confederate surgeons stayed behind on the fields of Gettysburg to help their wounded. Georgeanna Woolsey worked at a camp where soldiers spent the night before evacuation north, and she was amazed at how well wounded men from both sides got along.[111]

Cornelia provides her own, different, opinion of the medical work remaining at Gettysburg. She wrote: "We went—to one of the churches, where I saw for the first time what war meant. Hundreds of desperately wounded men were stretched out on boards laid across the high-backed pews so closely as they could be packed together. The boards were covered with straw. Thus elevated, these poor sufferers' faces, white and drawn with pain, were almost on a level with my own. I seemed to stand breast-high in a sea of anguish." Cornelia's group learned that wounded soldiers from the 12th Regiment of New Jersey were in a field hospital five miles outside of Gettysburg, and they headed there the next morning, expecting to find men they knew.

On July 8th she added: "There is a great want of surgeons here; there are hundreds of brave fellows, who have not had their wounds dressed since the battle. We have but one Rebel in our camp now; he says he never fired his gun if he could help it, and, therefore, we treat him first rate. I do not know when I shall go home—it will be according to how long this hospital stays here and whether another battle comes soon.

"I feel assured I shall never feel horrified at anything that may happen to me hereafter....Get the Penn. Relief to send clothing here; there are many men without anything but a shirt lying in poor shelter tents, calling on God to take them from this world of suffering.[112]

"In a tent where eight men lay with nothing but stumps—they call a leg cut off above the knee a 'stump'—they said if they held on a little longer they would form a stump brigade and go and fight them. We have some plucky boys in the hospital, but they suffer awfully." She also wrote home for the supplies most urgently needed, asking them to send pads to place under the wounded. Bandages she said were available in large quantities. The soldiers' mattresses were "filled with sticks and leaves,"[113] and so she pleaded for pads to protect bed-ridden patients and help heal their wounds. She also asked for dry rusk, a grain they could use to make bread that would keep for several days. At times she had no idea what day of the week it was. Cornelia also cared for one tent of "Johnnies" or Confederates but she was not obliged to give them anything but whisky.[114]

The expected follow-up battle never took place. General Meade had lost a fourth of the army to casualties, but reinforcements boosted the strength back to 85,000. Confederate losses, stragglers and deserters reduced their strength to 35,000 men. Immediately after the battle, however, the Union's "armed reconnaissance" mistakenly reported the Confederates were still strong in force and had not yet decided to give up the field. When the Confederates moved out, Union General Barlow, who was in the best position to judge, sent word that he believed the withdrawal was a "feint." Two other Union generals pushed forward and reported that the "enemy may have retired to take a new position and await an attack from us."[115]

A congressional committee investigated the Union's failure to pursue and destroy Lee's army. In the months and years that followed, Meade devoted many hours and wrote many pages defending his command decisions. On July 8, 1863, he wrote to his wife. "From the time I took command till to-day, now over ten days, I have not changed my clothes, have not had a regular night's rest, and many nights not a wink of sleep, and for several days did not even wash my face and hands, no regular food, and all the times in a great state of mental anxiety. Indeed, I think I have lived as much in this time as in the last thirty years."[116] Soldiers suffered that and much more, but General Meade writes, "The army is in fine spirits, and if I can only manage to keep them together, and not be required to attack a position too strong, I think there is a chance for me. However, it is all in God's hands."[117]

Many northerners criticized General Meade for too much caution and felt if he had pursued Lee he might have ended the war. By July 14, Lee's men rebuilt a bridge and crossed the Potomac River back onto Confederate soil. After the South moved away from Gettysburg, General Meade did not understand the great victory he had won.[118] If Lee had triumphed at Gettysburg, he could have moved on to Philadelphia, Baltimore and Washington. With Lee's aura of invincibility unbroken, Britain and France might have recognized the independent Confederacy. Instead Lee lost a third of his army, some 28,000 casualties, compared to 23,000 for the Union.[119]

Whatever a doctor's abilities, Union officers and enlisted men had little faith in the medical care they would receive. "If a fellow has to go to the hospital, you may as well say goodbye."[120] The authority of medical officers was weakened because everyone believed they played a temporary role.[121]

The sheer number of the dead and dying soldiers was unthinkable. Cornelia wrote that nearly 300 surgeons took five days to perform all the amputations required at Gettysburg, and many rebel soldiers were left to die on the battlefield with little food and untreated wounds.[122] Under these gruesome circumstances, she managed to earn respect from soldiers and medical staff.

While the Gettysburg battle still raged, Dr. Jonathan Letterman was ordered to establish a general hospital nearby to care for casualties at a single site. The struggle to care for casualties at Gettysburg are detailed in his report:[123]

"...The chief want was tents and other appliances for the better care of the wounded. I had an interview with the commanding general on the evening of July 3, after the battle was over, to obtain permission to order up the wagons containing the tents, etc. This request he did not think expedient to grant but in part, allowing one-half the wagons to come to the front; the remainder were brought up as soon as it was considered by him proper to permit it.

" Dr. [Henry] Janes, who was left in charge of the hospitals at Gettysburg, reports that quite a number of surgeons came and volunteered their services, but "they were of little use." This fact is so well known in this army that medical officers prefer to do the work rather than have them present, and the wounded men, too, are much better satisfied to be attended by their own surgeons. I, however, asked the Surgeon-General, July 7, to send 20 medical officers to report to Dr. Janes, hoping they might prove of some benefit, under the direction of the medical officers of this army who had been left behind. I cannot learn that they were ever sent.

" It is unnecessary to do more than make an allusion to the difficulties which surrounded this department at the engagement at Gettysburg. The inadequate amount of transportation; the impossibility of having that allowed brought to the front; the cutting off our communication with Baltimore, first by way of Frederick and then by way of Westminster; the uncertainty, even as late as the morning of July 1, as to a battle taking place at all, and, if it did, at what point it would occur; the total inadequacy of the railroad to Gettysburg to meet the demands made upon it after the battle was over; the excessive rains which fell at that time—all conspired to render the management of the department one of exceeding difficulty....

"...The conduct of the medical officers was admirable. Their labors not only began with the beginning of the battle, but lasted long after the battle had ended. When other officers had time to rest, they were busily at work—and not merely at work, but working earnestly and devotedly."

Another, more graphic account comes from Major General Carl Schurz:

> "To look after the wounded of my command, I visited the places where the surgeons were at work. At Bull Run, I had seen only on a very small scale what I was now to behold. At Gettysburg the wounded—many thousands of them—were carried to the farmsteads behind our lines. The houses, the barns, the sheds, and the open barnyards were crowded with the moaning and waiting human beings, and still an unceasing procession of stretchers and ambulances was coming in from all sides to augment the number of the sufferers. A heavy rain set in during the day—the usual rain after a battle and large numbers had to remain unprotected in the open, there being no room left under roof. I saw long rows of men lying under the eaves of the buildings, the water pouring down upon their bodies in streams. Most of the operating tables were placed in the open where the light was best, some of them partially protected against the rain by tarpaulins or blankets stretched upon poles.
> "   There stood the surgeons, their sleeves rolled up to the elbows, their bare arms as well as their linen aprons smeared with blood, their knives not seldom held between their teeth, while they were helping a patient on or off the table, or had their hands otherwise occupied; around them pools of blood and amputated arms or legs in heaps, sometimes more than man-high. Antiseptic methods were still unknown at that time. As a wounded man was lifted on the table, often shrieking with pain as the attendants handled him, the surgeon quickly

examined the wound and resolved upon cutting off the injured limb. Some ether was administered and the body put in position in a moment. The surgeon snatched his knife from between his teeth, where it had been while his hands were busy, wiped it rapidly once or twice across his blood-stained apron, and the cutting began."[124]

Cornelia zeroed in on the men. On July 7, 1863: "There are no words in the English language to express the suffering I witnessed today. The men lie on the ground; their clothes have been cut off them to dress their wounds. They are half naked, have nothing but hard tack to eat only as the Sanitary Commissions, Christian Association, and so forth give them. I was the first woman who reached the 2nd Corps after the three days fight at Gettysburg. I was in that corps all day not another woman within a half mile….I gave to every man that had a leg or arm off a gill of wine, to every wounded in Third Division, one glass of lemonade, some bread and preserves and tobacco—as much as I am opposed to the latter, for they need it very much, they are so exhausted.[125]

"I would get on first rate if they would not ask me to write to their wives; that I cannot do without crying, which is not pleasant to either party. I do not mind the sight of blood, have seen limbs taken off and was not sick at all." [126]

July 8th: "I believe the Government has possession of the road….One [patient] had his leg cut off yesterday, and some of the ladies, newcomers, were up to see him. I told them if they had seen as many as I had they would not go so far to see the sight again….The First Minnesota Regiment bears the first honors here for loss in the late battle….The Colonel I know well; he is a very fine man. He has three bullets in him; has had two taken out by Dr. Child, the other he got in at Antietam and it is there yet. I do hope he will recover." [127] Eighty-two percent of the First Minnesota soldiers were killed or wounded at Gettysburg—one of the highest casualty rates of the war.[128] The officer she refers to appears to be Colonel William Colville Jr., who survived his injuries.

Each evening after the fighting subsided, stretcher bearers and ambulances had collected wounded. An estimated 14,000 wounded men came to dressing stations and field hospitals during the battle. By the end of fighting in Gettysburg 20,342 wounded had to be treated.[129]

A surgeon who witnessed the revolution in medical care during the half century that followed described his Civil War experience in 1918: "We operated in old blood-stained and often pus-stained coats, the veterans of a hundred fights....We used undisinfected instruments from undisinfected plush-lined cases, and still worse, used marine sponges which had been used in prior pus cases and had been only washed in tap water. If a sponge or an instrument fell on the floor it was washed and squeezed in a basin of tap water and used as if it were clean. Our silk to tie blood vessels was undisinfected.... The silk with which we sewed up all wounds was undisinfected. If there was any difficulty in threading the needle we moistened it with...bacteria-laden saliva, and rolled it between bacteria-infected fingers. We dressed the wounds with clean but undisinfected sheets, shirts, tablecloths, or other old soft linen rescued from the family ragbag. We had no sterilized gauze dressing, no gauze sponges....We knew nothing about antiseptics and therefore used none. Gangrene, tetanus and other complications were so frequent that slight wounds often proved mortal."[130] No one understood that wounds should be kept clean. Infection too often ruined what otherwise was effective and appropriate treatment.

Blunt knives and saws were even more damaging than non-sterile equipment because poorly sharpened blades increased tissue damage. The surgeons' skill at sharpening instruments varied greatly.[131] Experience and necessity became great teachers, however.

Surgeons could not have performed the difficult operations they did without anesthesia. It would have been impossible to keep the patient in a quiet position during prolonged surgery, and the body would have gone into shock.[132] In Union field hospitals chloroform was almost uniformly used as anesthetic (76.2 percent of cases.) Ether was also used; in a small number of cases chloroform and ether were used in combination. In southern units chloroform was scarce.

Surgeons of the era thought the patient should be kept under just long enough to last through the severest part of the operation. The most common form of administering anesthetics was a cloth or paper folded in the shape of a cone, with a sponge in the apex, placed at some distance over the nose and mouth of the patient to allow the first inhalations to become diluted with air, and then gradually lowered to the nose until anesthesia was produced. Then the inhalation stopped. The method of a double fold of muslin over the mouth and nose of the patient and simply dropping the chloroform on it drop by drop was too tedious. Also, many operations were performed in the open air, and the drop method was avoided due to rapid evaporation.[133]

The number of lives that were saved because of anesthesia is impossible to determine. Statistics for making a comparison are nonexistent. Using anesthetics ended badly when they were improperly administered. Eighty medical records document patients who died while anesthetized.[134] One such case was Sergeant George S. Moss, Co. C, 125th New York, who received a shell wound of the penis, scrotum, and thigh at Gettysburg, July 3, 1863; the missile lodged in muscles at the back of the thigh. The patient wanted the bullet removed, but he refused to be touched without anesthesia. On August 8th a stimulant [alcohol] was given and chloroform administered; in one minute the patient came under its influence, the shell fragment was removed in less than half a minute, and additional stimulant administered. The patient's pulse became suddenly weak, and he died almost instantly. It was the opinion of surgeons present that the patient died from valvular [sic] affection of the heart.[135] The dates stand out—surgeons waited more than a month to attempt the operation, an incredible delay to modern readers.

Cornelia witnessed a case where the patient died under anesthesia, and the details match those surrounding Sergeant Moss's operation. She was present in Gettysburg on August 8th, and this adds to the likelihood she described his operation. When the patient died in a minute from the effects of chloroform, Cornelia wrote that nothing affected her as much since she had arrived. It seemed to her like "deliberate murder."[136] She also felt that when they had a good physician, orders came to promote, demote or remove him. Military matters were enough, she said, to aggravate a saint. "Everything possible was done to upset the wounded." The soldiers endured hardships she found impossible to explain to someone who didn't experience them.

The quantity of anesthetic administered varied widely: The smallest quantity was about two drams (1/8 of an ounce); the largest quantity of chloroform 96 drams, influenced by the length of the operation and surgeon's approach. Even after the war, administration of anesthetic was not exact.[137] Some surgeons prescribed alcohol as a stimulant prior to anesthesia; some avoided alcohol except in rare cases; some refused to give it altogether. Other physicians reserved alcohol until the middle or the end of an operation. Still other doctors gave alcohol in conjunction with "other restoratives" when they thought the patient suffered from extreme depression.

If a man survived surgery, blood poisoning was the next, significant hurdle. When many wounded men were placed on operating tables of field hospitals, they were covered in filth. They had marched for days, at times through swamps. Unless they could get off the battlefield on their own, some men languished for days before receiving treatment.[138] Hannah Ropes served behind the lines in Washington, D.C. as the chief nurse of Union Hospital. She witnessed the toll in human suffering. "When they first come in, they appear to gain because we feed them and tend so well their wounds, but soon the suppuration takes place then they get sad and lose their appetite."[139]

Blood poisoning killed more men, but soldiers were more afraid of gangrene. Caregivers helped spread gangrene from patient to patient. The treatment was to amputate the stump once more and pour hydrochloric or nitric acid on the wound, torturing the victim, racing to melt away the deadly tissue before the patient died. Gangrene remained a problem until mid-1864 when trial and error experimentation with solutions of bromine, a caustic chemical with properties close to chlorine and iodine, rapidly decreased hospital gangrene and made it rare by war's end.[140]

Civil War physicians learned that gangrene and skin infections, later known to result from streptococcus, were related and spread in the direction of hospital ventilation. This observation was correct because microorganisms can be scattered on air currents. Whenever possible, physicians isolated gangrene and skin infection patients together. The antiseptic value of carbolic acid had been described in 1860, and some surgeons applied it to dressings.[141] These precautions foreshadowed modern methods, but it wasn't until 1867 that Dr. Joseph Lister wrote his first article about his experiments with medical antiseptic.[142]

Little was known about what caused disease, how to stop it from spreading, or how to cure it. Surgical techniques ranged from barbaric to barely competent. A Civil War soldier's chance of dying was about one in four. An under-qualified, understaffed, and undersupplied medical corps cared for fallen men. However, the Union medical corps increased in size, improved its techniques, and gained a greater understanding of medicine and disease every year the war was fought. [143]

After two weeks of service at Gettysburg, Cornelia heard rumors that the field hospital would move. "The field hospital is a number of tents and nothing more." However, because she had struggled to put it into first-rate order, she was sorry to see it abandoned.

The soldiers under her care gave her a silver medal. "I received a few days ago, a Silver Medal worth twenty dollars. The inscription on one side is 'Testimonial of regard for ministrations of mercy to the wounded soldiers at Gettysburg, Pa.—July 1863.'" About the same period of time, she wrote, "There have been in the Corps Hospital I supposed some thirty women, and it seems I am the favored in the lot. Several, since they have seen mine [medal], have started a subscription for two other ladies. Most of the ladies are dead heads completely."[144]

At the end of July provisions gave out. They fed the wounded with dry bread and coffee, reducing the men to prayers and curses. The men expected hardship on the march and took their chances in battle. The idea of giving up one's life willingly for a noble cause was central to society. Men considered dying for their country the proper thing to do,[145] but when wounded and in the hospital they expected to have enough to eat, especially since they were deprived of it only through neglect or the inefficiency of officers in charge of stores.[146]

Whatever supplies got through came from the Christian Commission, Sanitary Commission and Ladies Aid. Cornelia described dark days, hard marching, poor fare and terrible fighting. Though she knew "the men were entitled to all the unemployed muscle that government and communities could provide," they endured one hardship after another, including starvation. She pledged her support "always and with unreserved good will."[147]

The third week of August the worst of the Gettysburg wounded died in rapid succession. Days before some men talked fervently about recovering but then turned to prayer to have the suffering end. One of the hardest tasks for Cornelia was to pack up belongings of a soldier who had died and return them to a girlfriend back home.[148] But also about this time, successful surgeries began to heal, and the medical staff started to get soldiers up and onto crutches.

She wrote many lines about the soldiers but rarely mentions her own hardships. At one point she admitted, "I wore all the skin off my toes marching so much."[149] Later on, "The rats gnawed my two hoods so they cannot be worn."[150] Instead of concentrating on her situation, Cornelia rejoiced in what she was able to accomplish. The staff called the woman in charge of clothing 'General Duncan' because she terrorized others in camp. Cornelia's ward was so clean Duncan "blew her sky high," charging Cornelia must get more than a fair share of supplies. If the men in her care were bedridden, but still could be patient and uncomplaining, Cornelia could hold her tongue and do whatever it took to make conditions better for them. Cornelia managed to get along with Duncan even though no one else did.[151]

She reported the patients talked "good politics." The view of the soldiers, however, differed from the verdict historians have reached. "McClellan is their man mostly," Cornelia wrote, and she had trouble understanding their loyalty to General George McClellan. In that respect, she glimpsed the conclusion of history. "The great exuberance of joy among the soldiers at the nomination of General McClellan is exasperating. It seems so stupid in them after all they suffered."[152] The men liked Meade because they thought he sympathized with McClellan. General Joseph Hooker, "Fighting Joe," was discredited in the men's eyes except that he fed them well—"a circumstance soldiers made great account of."[153] Cornelia offered her own opinions about men in command. "I detest war and officers, if you could know of the drunkenness and bearing of our major generals down here you would indeed feel disgusted with military officers.[154] General Hays …was so drunk in this last fight he could scarcely ride his horse."[155] When she described the conduct of enlisted men, however, she marveled at their dedication. "Many men who were not completely disabled wished to go back to the front as soon as they were well enough." [156]

"It is very beautiful, rolling country here; under favorable circumstances I should think it healthy, but now for five miles around, there is an awful smell of putrefaction." Cornelia Hancock, July 7, 1863.

Gettysburg National Military Park in 2009

A steady stream of ambulances transported the wounded men from the makeshift field hospitals to Camp Letterman, where each man was assigned to a bed in one of the large wards. This general hospital in Gettysburg was completed by mid-July and consisted of 500 hospital tents set in rows. Dr. Letterman became proficient at moving patients to larger hospitals as soon as they were able to travel. Cornelia recorded her emotions when the Second Corps field hospital closed and the wounded were taken to Camp Letterman. "It is like parting with one's own family, I go to see the boys and some cry that I cannot stay with them."[157]

In contrast to the much-needed help from the Sanitary Commission and other aid organizations, visits from curious civilians and politicians caused severe problems. A New York private wrote in 1862, "There is lots of ladies comes here to the Hospital, but they have not rubbed the skin off of any of the patients' faces yet." An Indiana volunteer, describing the various classes of visitors who flooded Washington hospitals in 1864, wrote: "First, and least important, are the wordy sympathizers—of both sexes. The male portion of these 'drones' are generally composed of broken-down, short-winded, long-faced, seedy preachers of all denominations. They walk solemnly up and down the wards, between the couches of patient sufferers; first casting their cadaverous looks and ghostly shadow upon all, and then, after a *whispered* consultation with the surgeon of the ward, offer to pray; do so, and retire, without having *smiled* on a single soldier or dropped a word of comfort or cheer. The females belonging to this [the first class] go gawking through the wards, peeping into every curtained couch…[and give] heart-rending outbursts of 'Oh, my Savior!…Only see what a horrid wound! Goodness, gracious, how terrible war is! my! my!! my!!! Oh, let's go— I can't stand it any longer!' And as they near the door, perhaps these dear creatures will wind up with an audible—'Heavens! what a smell! Worse than fried onions!'"[158] Cornelia agreed that fashionable ladies created a nuisance, noting, "I would like the Sect. of War…[to] make strict laws to keep ladies out."[159] If lady visitors heard the remarks soldiers made after they left, Cornelia felt more of them would have stayed away.

The Medical Department faced severe obstacles when trying to provide care. As previously outlined, they had problems with logistics, procurement, and funding. In addition, training for physicians and surgeons was primitive. In those days the country had 50 medical colleges, but literacy and academic standards were low. Any man who paid the matriculation fee could attend medical school despite a lack of qualifications.[160] Before the Civil War, a physician in the United States received minimal training. Nearly all older doctors had served as apprentices in lieu of formal education. Even if a doctor attended medical school, that did not guarantee he was well trained. The average American medical student attended two years or less, received practically no clinical experience, and was given virtually no laboratory instruction. [161]

The American Medical Association was established in 1847 and was trying to improve the standards to practice medicine and educate doctors, but few frontier students could fulfill more stringent requirements. This does not mean, however, that the best physicians were unaware of current medical information. Medical journals and army physicians' reports to the Surgeon General show that many doctors understood and were skilled at using diagnostic equipment like the stethoscope, microscope, clinical thermometer and ophthalmoscope. Surgeons knew they were part of a great historical event and made detailed records. Case histories show, for example, doctors could use a stethoscope to detect which lobe of a lung was diseased in ways equal to or better than modern physicians who now rely on technology.

Medical departments of both armies struggled to improve outcomes. The autopsies and research conducted during the Civil War resulted in clinical advances, such as tracheotomy, arterial ligation or tying major arteries, plastic surgery and neurosurgery.[162] If patients were going to die without intervention, surgeons made heroic attempts to save lives[163].

Assistant surgeons worked in field dressing stations, almost always within artillery range of the battle. Amputations were postponed until the patient came to the field hospital; only the most urgent operations were done at temporary depots. Performing surgery outdoors had two advantages: better lighting and a measure of safety in the administration of anesthesia. By October 1862 regulations required surgeons to consult with other physicians in all doubtful cases to prevent unnecessary surgeries, and only one in 15 physicians was allowed to operate.[164] However, surgery attracted many onlookers, and no one tried to spare the patients waiting in line. [165] The wounded watched what would happen when it was their turn to be hoisted onto the table.

Surgery to remove a bullet generally started when the surgeon inserted an unwashed finger into the wound.[166] Despite fearful odds nearly 75 percent of the war's 30,000 amputee patients survived.[167] Those results, achieved without X-rays, trained anesthesiologists, and so on, show that physicians were gaining knowledge and dexterity. The level of success doctors achieved is also a testament to the amount of injury and infection the human body can overcome.[168]

At the end of the war the best surgeons in the country were those with military experience. Dr. William Watson, who served as a Union surgeon, indicated, "on Sunday afternoon we were ordered to establish a hospital near the [Rappahannock] River. Here I saw more surgery than one would see in a whole lifetime of ordinary practice."[169] Cornelia gave examples of on-the-job training for surgeons. An hour after one leg amputation, "I saw one of the doctors cut it [the severed limb] into three pieces for the sake of practice."[170] She gave doctors high marks for dedication when they deserved them. "I will never say so much against any class of men as I did against surgeons [after I met the ones] this winter [who] have performed so faithfully."[171]

Dr. Jonathan Letterman was an innovator, who struggled to improve care. He has been called the Father of Modern Battlefield Medicine. In addition to improving ambulance services, Letterman standardized the way medicines and supplies were stocked in supply wagons and medical kits, making it possible for any physician to walk up to any wagon or kit, look in one specific place, and find exactly what he needed. Letterman also restructured medical command at the Division level and appointed the most qualified physicians to perform surgery, based on their lifetime experience, not on rank or length of military service.[172]

Even with the improvements Dr. Letterman put in place, the Gettysburg general hospital was an overwhelming place for anyone. Camp Letterman was filled to capacity by late July and eventually housed over 1,600 patients. Surgeons accomplished the amputation of an arm or leg in a matter of minutes and returned the soldier to his bed within the hour. Already weakened from the effects of wounds and surgery, patients also suffered the added effects of diarrhea and dysentery.[173]

Two months after Cornelia's arrival in Gettysburg, Dr. Child recommended that she take a month off. Cornelia disagreed. She felt the horrors of Gettysburg had been very hard on her brother-in-law Dr. Child, but she held up better. Nothing seemed like a hardship compared to the soldiers' lot. She didn't care where she was going to eat or sleep, not after all she had seen the soldiers bear patiently. Amid the suffering she witnessed, Cornelia also witnessed their lack of selfishness. Men grew quiet and patient with so much death nearby, often disregarding their own needs for the sake of a comrade. She followed their example and thought of others.

When Cornelia agreed to take a leave of absence, she did it for practical reasons. "By September the hospital got so full of women that one had to sit down while others turned round, so the most patriotic thing I could do was take my board off of Uncle Sam until there was a greater need."[174]

She anticipated how awful the next battle would be for she now knew many more men, and it would be harder than ever to see one of them hit. Less than 100 patients remained at Camp Letterman by November 10, 1863. It was officially closed a few weeks later. During a visit to her home, rural life seemed alien. Though the pull of family and friends remained strong, Cornelia now felt the stronger pull of public service. Her eyes were wide open to war's tremendous costs.

The time she spent in Gettysburg earned Cornelia a favorable reputation with some important people. The Governor of Pennsylvania Andrew Gregg Curtin invited Cornelia to attend the dedication of the Gettysburg cemetery on November 19, 1863. Even though the war was still raging, Governor Curtin had decided to consecrate 17 acres of ground. President Lincoln was also invited and came to say a few words to the crowd.

The smell of death hung in the air because workers were disinterring remains to give soldiers proper burials. The day of the ceremony a crowd filled Cemetery Hill. Cornelia recognized Secretary of War Stanton, who lifted his hat, smiled and bowed when he saw her. A number of the soldiers she had nursed back to health were there too, and she spent time reminiscing with "her boys." A hush fell over the crowd when President Lincoln and his party arrived.

Edward Everett was the main speaker, and he gave a two-hour passionate oration, filled with flawless intonation and gestures. When he finished, the applause was deafening.

Then President Lincoln added his words of consecration. Lincoln's speech was only 272 words. Various accounts indicate the crowd was quite surprised, when, after only two minutes, Mr. Lincoln sat down. When the day was over, Cornelia rode back to Washington, D.C. on one of the special trains added for the occasion. She tried to recall some of the elegant phrases of Mr. Everett's speech, but all she could remember were the face of Lincoln, his dark eyes, hollow cheeks, and the simple earnest words—"**that this nation, under God, shall have a new birth of freedom.**"[175]

Hospital for Former Slaves

After she witnessed the suffering at Gettysburg, Cornelia no longer wanted to live the quiet, submissive lifestyle typical for women of the era. The excitement and fulfillment of service turned inactivity into an "albatross," hanging around her neck. Contrary to the racism of the times, her attitude was to love all people equally. She changed to a job with an even lowlier status than that of volunteer nurse. In October 1863 she went to Washington to care for freed slaves, who were "everybody's headache and nobody's responsibility."[176]

The poor treatment African Americans received prompted her to write: "where are all those good abolitionists north that do so much talking and so little acting?" By November 5, 1863, the desperate conditions prompted her to cry out for aid: "My dear Sister

I shall depict our wants in true but ardent words, hoping to affect you to some action. Here are gathered the sick from the contraband camps in the northern part of Washington. If I were to describe this hospital it would not be believed." The term contraband came from Union General Benjamin Franklin Butler, who was a lawyer in civilian life.[177] Soon after Ft. Sumter three slaves crossed over to Union lines. Butler declared them contraband of war and refused to return them to their masters, as required by fugitive slave laws. Butler's action was hotly debated among Union officers, but the North increasingly came to the realization that they should deny the South the labor of slaves.

During the fall of 1863 newly freed slaves flooded into Washington, D.C. They desperately needed food, shelter and medical care. From the hospital where she worked, Cornelia wrote in January of 1864: "Smallpox has raged here to a great extent but a separate hospital has been established for that now."[178] And in a separate letter, "It is a miracle how any one can have prolonged good health in such a neighborhood. I supposed 10,000 rats would hardly cover the number that have lain unburied in our immediate vicinity for nearly one month.[179]

"[We need to have] men at the head of this bureau with living souls in them large enough to realize that a contraband is a breathing *human being* capable of being *developed,* if not so now. Let them have the power to appoint officers to have charge of these camps, good energetic, anti-slavery persons who will take an interest in the improvement of those under their charge. I feel this to be the duty of every individual to urge upon every senator and congressman that this step be taken, but meanwhile as we stand at present, our needs are very pressing.[180]

"[Senator Charles] Sumner is the handsomest man in the Senate. I had a conversation with him; he says the freedman's bureau will be established; says I must not be in a hurry, all things are coming round right."[181] But Cornelia had good reasons to want action. Conditions in camp were "revolting" with only one well, which was often out of order.

Cornelia could not understand how freed slaves managed to "keep body and soul together." The Office of American Freedman's Inquiry Commission set a tone that permitted deplorable conditions. In their preliminary report, dated June 30, 1863, the Commission stated: "Under any circumstances, and in all large societies, even during a normal and peaceful condition of things, there will be found a certain amount of vagrancy and a certain number of indigent poor, disabled, or improvident, to whom it is a custom and a duty to extend relief. Beyond this, except as an expedient for the time being, the Commission believes that the refugee freedmen *need no charitable assistance* [emphasis added.] In the city of Washington, containing 16,000 free colored persons, these support their own poor without almshouse aid, and scarcely a beggar is found among them.

"The vices chiefly apparent in these refugees are such as appertain to their former social condition. Men who are allowed no property do not learn to respect the rights of property. Men who are subjected to despotic rule acquire the habit of shielding themselves from arbitrary punishment by subterfuges, or by a direct departure from the truth. In the case of women living under a system in which the conjugal relation is virtually set at naught, the natural result is that the instinct of chastity remains undeveloped or becomes obscured."

In its final report of May 15, 1864, the Commission made an incredible, naïve assessment of what would happen: "There will for some time to come be a tendency on the part of many among those who have heretofore held them in bondage still to treat them in an unjust and tyrannical manner. The effectual remedy for this is, not special laws or a special organization for the protection of colored people, but the safeguard of general laws, applicable to all, against fraud and oppression.

"The sum of our recommendations is this: Offer the freedmen temporary aid and counsel until they become a little accustomed to their new sphere of life; secure to them, by law, their just rights of person and property; relieve them, by a fair and equal administration of justice, from the depressing influence of disgraceful prejudice; above all, guard them against the virtual restoration of slavery in any form, under any pretext, and then let them take care of themselves."[182]

Cornelia tried to inspire—or shame—others into providing relief for freedmen, women and children. "North of Washington, in an open, muddy mire, are gathered all the colored people who have been made free by the progress of our Army. Sickness is inevitable, and to meet it these rude hospitals, only rough wooden barracks, are in use—a place where there is so much to be done you need not remain idle. We average here one birth per day, and have no baby clothes except as we wrap them up in an old piece of muslin, that even being scarce.

"This hospital is the reservoir for all cripples, diseased, aged, wounded, infirm, from whatsoever cause; all accidents happening to colored people in all employs around Washington are brought here. It is not uncommon for a colored driver to be pounded nearly to death by some of the white soldiers. A woman was brought here with three children by her side; said she had been on the road for some time; a more forlorn, worn out looking creature I never beheld. Her four eldest children are still in Slavery, her husband is dead."[183]

When an ambulance driver tossed out five children infected with smallpox, Cornelia placed the children in a hospital tent and cared for them herself. At the contraband hospital between 40 and 50 new arrivals came each day, as the army advanced. The first priority for Cornelia was to vaccinate people against smallpox. After that, the needs were overwhelming. "Now this whole contraband business is under military regulation," she wrote, "and under officers that think to spend government money for contrabands all waste. Nothing…can be affected until the whole matter is removed from the military authority and vested in a bureau whose sole object is the protection and elevation of these people."[184] Cornelia lived from day to day and avoided thinking about what would happen next. She remained at the contraband facility until February 1864 when she returned to the battlefield.

The government's failure to address the "disgrace of prejudice" did not escape Cornelia. Her tour at the contraband camp left lasting impressions and prompted Cornelia to return to the plight of freed slaves after the war.

As long as combat raged, however, she wanted to serve near the battlefields. Cornelia showed the medal the soldiers at Gettysburg made for her to Senator Foster[g], who in turn presented the medal to Secretary of War, Edwin Stanton. February 10, 1864, she got her wish. "I start for the Army of the Potomac tomorrow morning. [Secretary of War] Stanton has granted me a permanent pass to visit anywhere in the lines of the Union army, which I regard as a great favor. It will save me much vexation among his sub-officials. My medal [from the soldiers at Gettysburg] secured it, and it was presented to him by Senator Foster…Soon after I received my pass I received a request from a Surgeon, requesting me to come immediately as they had 150 wounded just brought in.

"Direct letters in care of Dr. Dwinelle, Surgeon-in-Charge, 2nd Corps Hospital, near Brandy Station."[185] Although this new assignment meant hardship and danger, Cornelia regarded it as a reward for faithfulness.[186] She was eager to return to a corps hospital—and excitement of the frontlines.[187]

Winter Encampment

By 1864 war weariness turned public opinion against the war. At the beginning of the Civil War, most people had felt fighting would end by Christmas 1861. When that didn't happen, people believed that one decisive battle would determine the outcome; they relied on that fact—one overwhelming engagement, like Waterloo, would put an end to the carnage. No one envisioned the war would drag on for four years, ending when General Sherman's Union troops swept through Georgia and the Carolinas and General Grant engaged in trench warfare around Petersburg, Virginia.[188]

When Cornelia heard about northerners being vocal critics of the war, she couldn't contain her anger, "If it were not a mortal sin, I

---

[g] Cornelia does not indicate the Senator's full name. However, it appears she referred to the Republican Senator from Connecticut, Lafayette Sabine Foster

would say kill all the copperheads."[h] The government took steps to crush disloyalty. War opponents were arrested and held for months in military prisons without trial. General Ambrose Burnside issued a general order in 1863, which made it an offense to criticize the war in any way. Cornelia pushed aside political concerns, focused on the men under her care and what needed to be done to end hostilities. "It is now about nine o'clock, every tent has a light in it, and a lot of groaning sick men...I do not read the papers now...I look at it in this way that I am doing all a woman can do to help the war along."[189]

Most civilians couldn't fathom how difficult the enlisted man's life was. It angered soldiers to hear civilian men at home acting like arm-chair generals, as if they knew more than those at the front. When able-bodied men stayed home, it created ill will among the troops. Civilians in the North did well financially during the war, supplying ordinance and goods. Medical suppliers such as Edward R. Squibb and the Pfizer Company developed into pharmaceutical giants.[190] At the same time soldiers' families suffered from the lost wages or labor of the family breadwinner. Adjusting to war required men to face and overcome fear. Then soldiers had to come to terms with the moral burdens of killing countrymen. Soldiers wanted neighbors' support and wanted dissenters punished. Soldiers expected stay-at-homes to share the hardship.[191]

"I do not care what anyone says, war is humbug. It is just put out to see how much suffering the privates can bear."[192] Cornelia wrote those words February 24, 1864, to describe winter encampment at the field hospital at Brandy Station, Virginia. At this point she had been serving in Union hospitals for seven months. Brandy Station was within a few miles of the Union Army encampment. During the winter of 1863-64 Major General George G. Meade and the Union Army settled around Culpeper Courthouse in Virginia.

Commanders rarely gave furloughs. Privates spent three-quarters of their time in camp. Federal troops were often too far away to go

---

[h] Copperhead is a nickname given to a northerner who sympathized with the Secessionists of the South. The name refers to their angry, poisonous rhetoric.

home, while Southern armies, short of manpower, needed every available soldier and kept them on duty. As a result most soldiers stayed with their units for the duration of their enlistment.[193]

Even when soldiers were not engaged in battle, army camps were dangerous places. Exposure, malnutrition, and poor sanitation, all created incubators for disease. New regiments commonly had two-thirds of their men on the sick list. [194] Cornelia described the situation: "Our hospitals are full up…there is not shelter enough to keep them [the recruits] from winter. The consequence is they fall sick immediately and are carried here. I am quite busy, we have very sick men."[195]

Army medical officers performed a significant number of duties beyond their responsibility to the sick and wounded. They organized vast hospitals, equipped, supplied, and administered them, in addition to seeing sick and wounded by the thousands. Even surgeons with broad knowledge of military organization and methods had slim chances of meeting the overwhelming responsibilities.

The first duty for regimental surgeons each day was morning sick call. All the sick and disabled men trudged to the surgeons' tents for evaluation. A significant number of men feigned illness, and each surgeon had to decide which ones were faking. If a surgeon conducted the examinations carelessly, men evaded duty or men truly ill were returned to the ranks. When that happened, the surgeon fell into disgrace, which did not end with his tour of duty but followed him into civilian life.

After sick call the surgeon made hospital rounds and prescribed whatever medicines or diets were available. He inspected the camp daily and was responsible for keeping it well drained. If food in camp was not adequate, the surgeon was responsible for reporting it. Each of these duties was supposed to receive daily attention.[196]

Army officers made the surgeon's job more difficult because many of them were lax about sanitation. Some commanders refused to accept responsibility for their men's bathing and diet. They viewed these duties as unbecoming. Soldiers were supposed to bathe once a week, but many men and officers ignored the order. Latrines were uncovered, shallow trenches. Clothing and shelter were inadequate.

Lack of vegetables added to the sick roles, slowed down recovery from illness and wounds, and added to mortality rates.

Disease was a more formidable killer than guns, bayonets or canons. Approximately 620,000 men—360,000 Northerners and 260,000 Southerners—died in the four-year conflict, more fatalities than all other wars America fought. Various sources indicate 2.1 million Union soldiers and 880,000 Confederates took up arms from 1861-5. A death toll of 600,000 represented 2 percent of the country's total population and the equivalent of six million deaths based on today's population. Most men died due to illnesses—for the Union, roughly three out of five died of disease, and for the Confederacy an estimated two out of three died from disease. On the one-year anniversary of starting to the army, Cornelia wrote to her sister that "There are very few wounded left here now, mostly sick." At that point she was at City Point, where the cannonading "was incessant, but very few are wounded by it."[197]

Slipshod recruiting contributed to the staggering number of illnesses. Under- or over-age men and those in poor health were allowed to join up. Outbreaks of measles, chickenpox, mumps, and whooping cough plagued the ranks. When it came to communicable diseases, the first to strike usually was measles. Complications from lack of shelter led to pneumonia. New recruits from rural areas were susceptible to measles and mumps because they had not acquired the immunity, which protected soldiers who came from densely populated urban areas.

The winter of 1864-5 was the harshest of the era adding to the number of respiratory infections.[198] Men feared the ague (malaria) more than facing the enemy. Less prevalent but more deadly was typhoid. Many soldiers died from tuberculosis. The main culprit of wartime illness, however, was the shocking filth in the camp.[199] The most frequent ailment mentioned in soldiers' letters was diarrhea or dysentery. About half of the deaths from disease during the Civil War were caused by intestinal disorders, mainly typhoid fever, diarrhea, and dysentery.[200]

When infection or epidemics were not decimating the ranks, sunstroke was—especially among recruits who had not learned how to protect themselves by dropping out of the line if necessary. Both soldiers and medical staff suffered from:

> Chronic Diarrhea—Diarrhea was a symptom of dysentery.
>
> Typhoid fever—A gastrointestinal condition caused by a bacterial infection, usually as a form of food poisoning.[i]
>
> Typhus—Infectious fever characterized by high temperature, headache, and dizziness and a general name for various parasite infections, usually spread by insect bites.
>
> Smallpox—The policy to vaccinate all recruits, not previously inoculated, was not enforced.[201] Whenever possible smallpox cases were isolated in special hospitals called "pest houses."
>
> Yellow Fever—Yellow fever is a mosquito-borne viral disease. Illness ranges in severity from an influenza-like syndrome to hepatitis and hemorrhagic fever.[202]

The toll disease took forced combat units and medical personnel to do what they should have done at the outset—improve hygiene.[203] Discipline improved after the first two years—and then so did the health of the troops.

Physicians learned a number of lessons that transformed the practice of medicine. They found out daily doses of quinine prevented malaria. They began to abandon the practice of blood-letting or bleeding patients because they discovered that it was of no value in the treatment of diseases that ran a natural course like measles or, for that matter, many other diseases. Doctors also learned that strict quarantine prevented the spread of infections such as yellow fever.[204] The concept of contagion was controversial at this point in history. Quarantine was still being debated scientifically and, because it restricted liberty, was unpopular. The exception was smallpox, which was known to be contagious.[205] President Lincoln became an interesting exception to the isolation of smallpox patients. He had a mild case of smallpox after his speech at Gettysburg but was allowed to rest and recover in the White House.[206]

---

[i] Typhoid fever is unrelated to typhus, which is a tick-borne infection.

As bad as conditions were for Union troops, things were worse for Confederates. Druggists in the South had to manufacture what they could from native barks, leaves, herbs and roots, or purchase whatever supplies the blockade runners brought to southern ports. In most cases these cargoes were offered at auction at Galveston, New Orleans, Mobile, Charleston, Pensacola, Savannah, and Wilmington. The Gulf cities received supplies from Cuba, while in Texas there was almost a continuous train of smugglers, bringing goods across the Rio Grande from Mexico. The excessive price of quinine to treat malaria made smuggling it highly profitable.[207]

Dr. J. Julian Chisholm, Professor of Surgery in the Medical College of South Carolina, published a *Manuel of Military Surgery for the use of the Surgeons in the Confederate Army* in 1861. This book was widely used and a valuable contribution to war surgery. It contained a collection of hints and instructions about treating sick or wounded men in camp, on the field of battle and in the hospital. In his preface he wrote in part: "As our entire army is made up of volunteers from every walk in life, so we find the surgical staff of the army composed of physicians without surgical experience. Most of those who composed the staff were general practitioners, whose country circuit gave them but little surgery and seldom presented a gunshot wound. Moreover, as our country had been enjoying an uninterrupted state of peace, the collecting of large bodies of men and retaining them in health, or the hygiene of armies, had been a study without an object and therefore of little interest."

Treatments were traditional homeopathic remedies: For rash they used red-oak bark and alum. Goose grease and sorghum, or honey, was a standard remedy for croup, backed up with turpentine and brown sugar. Sassafras tea was given as a blood medicine. Colds were doctored with horsemint tea and tea from the roots of broom sedge. For rashes and impure blood, spice-wood tea was given. Mutton suet, sweet gum and the buds of the balm of Gilead was a standard salve for all cuts and sores. Balsam cucumber was widely used as a tonic and a remedy for burns. For hemorrhages, black haw root was commonly used. For diarrhea, roots of blackberry and blackberry cordial and a tea made from the leaves of the rose geranium.[208] Soldiers knew that blackberries were medicinal. Blackberry Balsam had been used to cure diarrhea since the 1840s and continued to be used for 120 years. General William Tecumseh Sherman indicated "an entire skirmish line, without orders, will fight a respectable battle for possession of an old field of blackberries."[209]

Streams used for drinking water were a source of disease and death. In the absence of effective medicines, intestinal disease remained widespread. Dr. Cowan, a physician to a Tennessee regiment, devised what became a famous tablespoon remedy, consisting of a tablespoon of Epsom salts, and equal quantities of bicarbonate soda and laudanum, dissolved in water and taken a tablespoonful at a dose. His remedy acted magically and attracted the notice of General Nathan Bedford Forrest, who, out of admiration and gratitude, promoted Dr. Cowan to his personal staff with the rank of major.[210]

For five months during the winter of 1863-4, both sides studied each other, reinforced their armies, and tested each other's lines with occasional thrusts. President Lincoln appointed Grant commander of all Union armies on March 9, 1864, and General Grant arrived in Virginia that same month. When Grant took command of the Army of the Potomac, all civilians were ordered to leave. Cornelia's letters from Brandy Station, Virginia, continue until April 12, 1864. After that, she returned to Philadelphia, but only for a short time. Soon she would disregard regulations—and slip back into action.

Return to Fighting

On May 5, 1864, Cornelia was walking on a street in Philadelphia when she heard news about the Battle of the Wilderness. The Union crossed the Rapidan River on May 4, 1864, and the headlines told of General Hays, who was killed by a bullet through the head on the first day. Cornelia immediately headed to Washington where she appealed to Secretary of War Edwin Stanton for a pass. Because confusion and uncertainty reigned, Stanton refused her request. To get around the restriction, Cornelia asked Dr. Child to take her along as an assistant. Each physician was allowed to take one aide. Together they went by steamboat to Belle Plain.

The war in Virginia was about to enter a prolonged, bloody phase. Grant's unrelenting pursuit of the Confederates would result in 45 percent casualties for each army within two-and-a-half months.[211] Historians indicate General Grant wept after the Battle of the Wilderness. Yet he doggedly kept Union troops pursuing victory. Throughout the summer until October 1864, the armies continued to cut and thrust, skirmishing almost daily. In these weeks of fighting, the Union did not gain a clear-cut victory over General Lee's army, but doctors and nurses saw no let up of hospital duty.[212]

Military historian Wayne Motts described the Civil War as an infantryman's war. In previous conflicts like the Mexican War, soldiers carried smoothbore muskets, which were inaccurate unless fired at close range. By the Civil War weaponry had gotten better. The infantry now carried rifled muskets with grooved rifle barrels that improved accuracy even at distances. Sharpshooters were able to place 10 shots in a 10-inch circle from 200 yards. The ability to hit the target from a distance proved deadly. When an infantry held a defensive position, they decimated any line of soldiers charging forward. No matter how disciplined or how many men massed up, the rifled musket cut men down, and elongated, soft lead bullets created dangerous, crushing wounds. Civil War infantries inflicted 91 percent of the casualties while only nine percent came from artillery. Later on, in World War I for example, 70 percent of casualties came from artillery fire.[213]

"A March in the Ranks, Hard-Prest and the Road Unknown"
by Walt Whitman, who cared for wounded at Fredericksburg.

Surgeons operating, attendants holding lights, the smell of ether,
*   the odor of blood;*
The crowd, O the crowd of the bloody forms—the yard outside also
*   fill'd;*
Some on the bare ground, some on planks or stretchers, some in
*   the death-spasm sweating;*
An occasional scream or cry, the doctor's shouted orders or calls;
The glisten of the little steel instruments catching the glint of the
*   torches;*
These I resume as I chant—I see again the forms, I smell the
*   odor;*
Then hear outside the orders given, Fall in, my men,
Fall in;

When she rejoined the Army, Cornelia felt as if she "had got back home." The surgeon who "sent a positive request for her to come" was Dr. Frederick Dudley, who remembered her from Gettysburg. He had been wounded in the shoulder, and she "carried him grub" on the battlefield. The surgeon in charge of the new hospital was Dr. Dwinelle, but Dr. Dudley was in charge of the Third Division. Records don't give Dr. Dudley's side of the story, but it seems he was glad to see Cornelia for personal reasons as well as professional ones. He made sure a log house was built for her and sent for a stove to warm her quarters. [214]

Field hospitals consisted of large tents, which accommodated from 20 to 25 men. The tents were usually put up in a shady part of the camp; the inside was leveled, and board floors laid, if boards could be procured. Sometimes straw ticks and cot bedsteads were available, but not in sufficient quantity to supply all the hospitals. Along each side of the tent the sick were laid, on blankets or cots, leaving room to pass between them. A temporary board table for books, medicines and supplies stood in the center of the tent. Surgeons visited patients twice every day, more often if required. The hospital steward filled prescriptions, and nurses administered the medicines.

When not on duty in the hospital, male nurses spent time digging drains around the tents. Draining the grounds was a vital part of hospital duty. Without ditches for drainage when thunderstorms came, it was impossible to keep tent floors from flooding. At times rain came down in torrents or strong winds threatened to lift tents off the ground, and everything fell into wild confusion.[215]

John G. Perry, an assistant surgeon for the Union Army, provided an account of his efforts to save a captain from his wounds—and then from drowning. While on maneuvers Perry spotted a pair of boots sticking out of a clump of bushes. He pulled Captain Kelliher out and found he was horribly mangled about the face and neck, bleeding from a lacerated artery. Perry stopped the hemorrhage by tying the vessel; Kelliher was placed on a stretcher and carried to the rear. At the division hospital the surgeon removed a shattered lower jaw, the whole arm including shoulder blade and clavicle and two ribs. Before surgery the surface of the lung was exposed, afterward the sutures ran from the ear to almost the pelvis. Hope that he would survive was nonexistent. Perry placed the captain in his own tent and told the steward how to care for the patient. During the night it rained so hard that Perry dug a trench around Kelliher to keep him from being drenched. The following day the troops were ordered to push on and place those unable to march on wagons. Perry asked Captain Kelliher if he wanted to stay behind and risk capture. His prompt reply was that he would go, "and, Doctor, I shall live." Perry never dreamed he would survive, but Captain Kelliher recovered, rejoined his regiment, was commissioned as a major, and served until the end of the war.[216]

Cornelia responded to the need for nurses in Spotsylvania County, Virginia. Battles between Grant's Army of the Potomac and Lee's Army of Northern Virginia raged there for almost three weeks. During this campaign, "nothing was to be seen but the densest clouds of smoke, a burning slave pen and ruins."[217] On May 11, 1864 Cornelia went to Belle Plain, where many of the men had been badly burned because the woods had been on fire. In this instance a letter from Dr. Child to his wife Ellen described what they found. "I was set to work at once placing the wounded men on the boat [the Wawasset]. More than 3,000 were sent to Washington this afternoon [May 12]...We put up tents & got a fire going & Cornelia was the first and only woman there yesterday."[218] He left Cornelia, working on the wharf. At 10 o'clock at night Dr. Child finished and went back to look for Cornelia, but she had gone.

Her letter for this date stated, "On going ashore at Belle Plain we were met with hordes of wounded soldiers who had been able to walk from the Wilderness battlefield to this point....Soon the long train of ambulances containing severely wounded men commenced arriving and among them the Head Qts. Ambulance with Gen. Hays' dead body on its way to Pittsburg. I knew this ambulance had to report back to the 2nd Corps Hospital." Cornelia got onto the ambulance with two surgeons headed for the return trip, stating that she rode with Dr. Detmold and Dr. Vanderpool, who were from New York. When they arrived at the front, "The scenes beggared all description and these two men, eminent as they are in their profession, were paralyzed by what they saw. Rain had poured through the bullet-ridden roofs of the churches until our wounded lay in pools of water made bloody by their seriously wounded condition." Cornelia explained that the surgeons gazed in horror and did not seem to know where to begin.

She relied on her Gettysburg experience and was able to "take hold." After the surgeons got through the first, horrible day, on the second day they had church pews taken apart. The backs and seats were then raised off the floor on cleats to keep the wounded from lying in the water. After this, Cornelia reported, "An amputating table is improvised under a tree in the yard where these two good men work indefatigably."[219]

Soldiers from both sides remembered May 12, 1864, as one of the darkest days of the war. Confederates set the stage on the evening of May 11 when they removed their artillery under the mistaken impression that Grant had moved away. However, Union General

Winfield Scott Hancock's[i] corps spent the rainy night sloshing into position to launch a massive strike. That attack began about dawn and succeeded in capturing many of the Confederates. Ironically, the magnitude of Hancock's victory retarded his progress. Nearly 20,000 soldiers milled about gathering prizes, escorting captives to the rear, and generally losing their organization and drive.

The delay provided the South an opportunity, and Confederates managed to restore all but a few hundred yards of the original southern line. The Union Sixth Corps now joined the fray, and for the next eighteen hours horrifying close-quarters combat spilled blood on both sides. The fighting focused on a slight bend in the works, known to history as the Bloody Angle. A shallow valley sliced close to the Confederate line at this point, providing crucial shelter for swarms of Union soldiers. An appalling pattern developed. Federals left the cover of the forest, crossed the road and took refuge in the swale. From there they maintained a constant rifle fire and made periodic lunges onto the works at the Bloody Angle. The battle assumed an unspeakable character all its own, unrelated to strategy and tactics or even victory and defeat. "The horseshoe was a boiling, bubbling and hissing cauldron of death," wrote a Union officer. "Clubbed muskets, and bayonets were the modes of fighting for those who had used up their cartridges, and frenzy seemed to possess the yelling, demonic hordes on either side."[220]

The surgeons and Cornelia had wanted to travel as far as Fredericksburg, Virginia, but southern guerrillas were too great a threat, and they were delayed. A cavalry escort got the party through, and once in Fredericksburg, "The news is very rejoicing this morning, but we never believe anything here. Suffering, suffering, but the men are in good spirits as we appear to be gaining." Cornelia was the first Union woman in Fredericksburg, Virginia. There she chartered a new hospital. Other hospitals in town, she reported, were "shocking in filth and neglect. Ours is the best. I wish all in Fredericksburg and beyond were as comfortable as ours."[221]

---

[i] Prior researchers indicate no family relationship between General Winfield Scott Hancock and Cornelia Hancock.

Battlefield conditions were not good for the Union, "Our whipped cavalry huddled behind the breastworks, both horses and men, looking in the most exhausted condition."[222] The devastation pushed aside all her other concerns. "I have lost all interest in political affairs, have no eyes, ears, for anything but the sufferings of soldiery....I dressed wounds; there were not surgeons enough willing to stay in the sun...and it was too awful to leave them uncared for...Such tired agonized expressions no pen can describe...By the time one set were got in and comfortable another set would arrive so it went for two weeks."[223] Cornelia remained in Fredericksburg until May 28, 1864.

In comparison to Cornelia's descriptions, General Grant's accounts are workmanlike. About this period he indicates, "Lee had weakened the other parts of his line...and I determined to take advantage of it." Grant explained troop movements in great detail. When discussing the human cost, however, he typically described the casualty rates in two-word bits. He described the men killed or maimed as "great slaughter" or "heavy loss." At one point of the ongoing battle, he wrote, "So much time was lost in trying to get up the troops which were in the right position to reinforce, that I ordered Upton to withdraw; but the officers and men of his command were so adverse to giving up the advantage they had gained that I withdrew the order...[The subsequent assault] was gallantly made, many men getting up to, and over, the works of the enemy; but they were not able to hold them. At night, they were withdrawn."[224]

Military tactics like these disgusted Cornelia. "The idea of making a business of maiming men is not worthy of a civilization." She acknowledged General Grant's concern for the men, however. "Grant walks round the hospit[al] quite frequently,"[225] and she deferred to the opinions soldiers held about their commander. "U.S. Grant is creating great activity in the Army now; he is bringing out heavy artillery, men who have been lying around Washington, arming them ...and bringing them to the front. That gratifies the inmost souls of these veterans."[226] As the carnage continued, she concluded,

"I do not see Grant has accomplished much, yet he fights right straight ahead whether he gets any advantage or not."[227]

On May 20, 1864, from Fredericksburg: "I hope the North does not feel jubilant over our successes for we have little cause so far. It seems to be Grant's determination to persist if he is whipped, and I can assure anyone he is whipped about half the time but he does not appear to care. The suffering does not seem so great as at Gettysburg because they [the wounded] are in houses."

She also documented that one of their physicians, Dr. Aiken, was taken prisoner for two weeks but released on May 20, 1864. "I tell you I was glad. He is nearly starved."[228] Many doctors displayed heroism: throughout the war 32 medical corpsmen were killed in battle, nine died by accident, 83 wounded, 290 died of disease, and four died in Confederate prisons.[229] Surgeons technically were classified as non-combatant, yet they were captured and held in military prisons like other personnel. Medical officers often faced the hard choice of deserting wounded who urgently needed attention or remaining and risking capture with all the misery imprisonment entailed. General Thomas J. "Stonewall" Jackson captured the Federal division hospitals in May 1862 and took the position that surgeons did not make war and should not suffer its penalties; he returned them unconditionally to their own forces. The neutral status of surgeons was formally agreed upon between Generals McClellan and Lee, but as hostilities dragged on their agreement later broke down.

Union forces advanced on Richmond but stalled at Spotsylvania Court House on May 8th during a two-week series of battles. A Union attack on May 12 and 13, 1864, captured nearly a division of Lee's army and came near to cutting the Confederate army in half. Confederate counterattacks plugged the gap, and fighting continued for nearly 20 hours in what has been called the most ferociously sustained combat of the Civil War. On May 19, a Confederate attempt to turn the Union right flank was beaten back with severe casualties. On May 21, Grant disengaged and continued his advance on Richmond.[230] On June 9th Cornelia wrote, "I suppose the North is clamoring 'on to Richmond' still, but I fear it will be some time yet before the clamor will cease."[231]

General Grant's memoir confirmed he created activity and turned field commanders lose with orders to strike. In the early days of June 1864, the Union captured Old Cold Harbor in Virginia. The Confederates were determined that the Union would not hold onto this valuable area and counterattacked. Grant writes that Confederate attacks were repulsed but Union Commanders "did not follow these up as they should have. I was so annoyed at this that I directed Meade to instruct his corps commanders that they should seize all such opportunities when they occurred, and not wait for orders."[232] Though Grant described encounter after encounter as causing heavy losses, he urged officers to press the enemy relentlessly.

Though no one could predict what might happen so close to the front, Cornelia downplayed the danger she faced. After the wounded men were evacuated to Washington, the Union pulled out of Fredericksburg, and Cornelia went with the troops. "The men prepared for march, about 8,000, are all in line with shining bayonets. The cavalry, all mounted officers, riding up and down the line, flags waving, everything around is exhilarating. A courier who just brought in a dispatch from Gen. Grant is guarding our wagon. [He is] the most splendid rider I ever saw and is as brave as can be. He had his horse shot under him but soon captured another."

During the forced march, men "are constantly falling by the roadside. I have carried lots of their guns and knapsacks for them today. I felt many times like giving them my seat."[233] The end of May no passes were granted to women—except to return to Washington—yet Cornelia left Port Royal and joined the march for White House, Virginia, a distance of 45 miles. She heard that women would not be allowed—but that did not stop her. "I sat upon my trunk perfectly easy. There has always been a way provided and I always expect there will be, so never concern. At length a doctor comes up who volunteers us to go on the transport without a pass. That I often do. But I like going in the wagon train better and the Sanitary have offered to carry us thru, so now I am sitting in their wagon."[234]

Along the way, "There is almost always an alarm along the line about Guerillas," she wrote, "often just enough to make a pleasant excitement. I cannot feel afraid and strange as it may seem the soldiers want to have a brush with them."

She reported being able to sleep well among the enemy. "The army has never passed through this neighborhood...at night we halted at a village called Newton, went into a Secesh house, found a nice bed to sleep in but they say they have nothing to eat, sent back to the train for rations and had the colored people to get us a good supper which we ate upon their table. The women are bitter Secessionists—one said her husband is a commissary in the Rebel army. We think he furnishes rations to the guerilla band and I was not disposed to show them any favours [sic] but true to some people's idea of right they wanted to take Sanitary supplies and give [to] those rebels to live on because they said they were starving. Guarding Secesh property is entirely played out with me.

"June 1st, this morning we left our Secesh enemies and resumed the march. It is extremely dusty. About a mile on the road when the guerillas made a dash but quicker than a flash our cavalry drove them in the woods. I never saw anything more firmly accomplished."[235]

After several weeks at White House Landing, Cornelia had made her way to City Point, Virginia, which served as Grant's supply depot during the siege of Petersburg. City Point would become one of the most extensive hospitals the government organized. The scene was a confusion of cannon, cattle, contrabands, rebels, and boys in blue.

While in City Point, medical personnel came under fire. Cornelia was among those who had to be rapidly evacuated. In the melee, one party of officers "had their horses in our way...[Cornelia] had to startle them and run under their heads to pass....What a monstrous body of men a cavalry is, jaded in countenance, covered in dust."[236] Also at City Point, she wrote, "What a sight it is to see them [men I know]. It is a privilege all enjoy—to kill themselves." [Captain Charles H. Dod] "put all his dependence on my energies in this world and the Savior for the next....I expect now soon to be the only remnant of our Corps left."[237] Correspondence between the Dod family and Cornelia after the war later showed Captain Dod truly felt he owed Cornelia a great debt.

The Union had seven hospitals in City Point. The largest, where Cornelia worked, was the Depot Field Hospital which covered nearly 200 acres and could hold up to 10,000 patients. Even though she was stationed a mile away from Grant's headquarters, the cannonading was "perfectly deafening and sickening when you know what a scene it would bring."[238] There were twelve hundred tents and ninety log barracks. Late in summer of 1864 Cornelia described her quarters as comfortable and her workload as manageable. However, the duty was always worrisome. In August of 1864 she had 183 low diet patients,[239] which meant the doctors ordered nourishment in the form of wine, whey, milk and water, rice gruel, always something very light because the men were not strong enough for solid food.

Cornelia remained at City Point until the end of the war. General Grant kept the pressure on the Confederates and gradually depleted their lines. Ultimately the South could not replace their losses. On April 3, 1865, she wrote: "This morning we could see the flames of Petersburg lighting the skies. The wounded are constantly coming in. I shall probably be one of the first Union women in Richmond." Petersburg saw the armies use large-scale entrenchments for the first time—in an eerie preview of World War I.

On April 11, 1865: "Lee has now surrendered. A bloodless surrender keeps our hospital still empty, and we have time to give attention to a few who are dying just when they want most to live. I shall come home when the 12th New Jersey is mustered out of the service. I am well and very busy finishing up this Rebellion."[240]

President Lincoln visited their hospital after Richmond fell, and Cornelia was on hand to record the event. "The medical directors wanted to call his [Lincoln's] attention to the appointments of the hospital but [instead] he shook hands with the men who were able to stand in line and went to the bedsides of those unable and spoke to them."[241]

For the entire conflict, Union records show that medical staff treated 5,825,480 cases of wounds and disease among the white troops and 629,354 cases among the colored troops.[242] Detailed records for the Confederacy were lost to fire. By the end of the war, nurses had proved themselves indispensable, and the medical establishment supported civilian nursing schools for women.[243] Successes during the Civil War also encouraged sanitation in American cities. The Civil War created an acceptance in American society of government intervention and action. In 1866 when a cholera epidemic hit New York, it led to the creation of the New York Board of Health charged with cleaning up the city, disinfecting the homes of victims and providing clean water.[244]

Cease Fire

Demobilization began immediately; 800,000 soldiers retired in six months.[245] Troops marched past President Johnson's reviewing stand for two days in Washington, D.C. "A spectacle," wrote the *New York Tribune,* "as no other continent saw, as this continent will never see again."

Cornelia was invited to Washington for the two-day celebration in May 1865. She described the scene, "On the first day's review in Washington, I saw the Army of the Potomac from the piazza of a country house where I could speak to those I knew. When Sherman's army passed I was on the President's Grand Stand and saw General Sherman as he passed from the Treasury Building to the White House—the only moving figure—he was mounted on a fine black horse, with all the bands playing."[246] After the greatest parade in United States history, she returned to Hancock's Bridge to visit her parents, brother Will, friends and neighbors.

When soldiers returned home, extravagant expressions of support for the troops turned into hollow words. No provision had been made for the disabled. Only a pitifully small number of returning veterans found work due to an alarming unemployment rate. Employers discriminated against veterans because they thought army life ruined a man's character.[247] The veteran's movement started because they needed relief from the intolerable employment situation and to raise funds for the disabled.[248] The Grand Army of the

Republic veteran's organization created a powerful lobby for pensions, but it also provided relief at local posts, giving food, coal, loans, jobs, free medical care, rent, and stipends for widows and schools for orphans.[249]

The Hancock family farm was never more beautiful. The placid stream and scent of the tidewater marsh stirred Cornelia deeply. Family members were eager to hear her experiences, but Cornelia could not talk openly about what she'd been through. Her answers were evasive.[250] Quiet, country life left her restless. She stayed in Hancock's Bridge only for a few days and then went to Philadelphia to stay with her sister Ellen and Dr. Child. Their home was a center for Quaker thought and activity and site of the Race Street Yearly meeting.[251] Cornelia quickly became involved in discussions about Reconstruction and the reforms being proposed by civic-minded men and women.

Rebuilding society was as monumental an undertaking as the war had been. The horrendous death toll had continued for four years. Casualty rates were thirty percent in battle after battle.[252] Some towns lost an entire generation of young men. According to Civil War historian Shelby Foote, "The Civil War defined us as what we are, and it opened us to being what we became—good and bad things."[253] Foote believed that any understanding of our nation should be based on "the enormous catastrophe" of the Civil War. The national struggle, in his words, provided the "crossroads of our being." Even after the South's formal surrender, America faced severe tests. Numerous historians have explained how the Civil War forever changed warfare, medicine, government and society. At the end of hostilities the federal government was once more unprepared—and unable to prevent further tragedy.

Generals wrote their memoirs, and the books became best-sellers. Veterans were eager to understand the roles they had played in the marathon drama. Individual army units could then point to places they held off large assaults. Unlike trench-bound or continually bombarded soldiers of future wars, the actions of individual units changed the course of large battles.[254] Stately memoirs played down the carnage of battle. Officers concentrated on troop movements and filled pages with military strategies rather than depict the human toll. George Meade and David Sickles debated the tactics of each general at Gettysburg in lengthy prose. The confusion and bloodshed tended to disappear from accounts. General Grant wrote a two volume memoir, which evaded the simmering hatreds. Grant barely touched upon issues with critical postwar implications, such as the burning of Atlanta. When he described the city's capture, his memoir merely stated, "The city of Atlanta was turned into a military base. The citizens were all compelled to leave. Sherman also very wisely prohibited [traders]…from trading with the citizens."[255]

Even foot soldiers' accounts focused on locating themselves in the panorama of the campaigns or rejoicing that they did their part in re-establishing the Union, "the land of the free and the home of the brave. All honor to the boys in blue."[256] Cornelia's letters have qualities the grand memoirs lack, providing more balance—detailing failures as well as successes, and brutality as well as goodness.

Cornelia had learned strategic lessons. Experience became a proving ground. Like other women who remained long enough to get to know the soldiers, she began to think of herself as one of the men's comrades.

In the nineteenth century, American men focused on the power of the individual. Men were fond of terms like self-respect, self-cultured, and self-educated. Henry Clay coined the intoxicating, long-lasting phrase "self-made." For men of his era the emphasis was not just on wealth or social status but on developing their potential. They devoted time and energy to discipline and character; they remade themselves with the idea self-improvement was the first step toward remaking the world.[257] In a study of self-made men, Joyce Appleby concluded the host of new opportunities transformed, not only men, but society as a whole. Many young men left home and tried new careers. Instead of following the traditional paths of parents and ancestors, young innovators broke free, faced significant risks and pursued new lifestyles. "The range and sweep of enterprise in this period are awesome," Appleby concluded, "suggesting the widespread willingness to be uprooted, to embark on an uncharted course of action, to take risks with one's resources—above all the resource of one's youth."[258] The kernel of success lay within the individual rather than society or a family. Ralph Waldo Emerson summed up men's attitudes, "the reason why this or that man is fortunate is not to be told. It lies in the man; that is all anybody can tell you about it." Like men of the era, Cornelia had become self-made in the best sense of the words.

Going out into the world was a great risk, especially for a young woman, but she became more independent and assertive than many female counterparts—at the same time avoiding confrontations with the male establishment. She was not a feminist but a proponent of human dignity for all. When authorities ignored or refused her, she slipped past regulations or turned the rules to her favor. Hers was a delicate balancing act, pushing forward in a fervent desire to help and pulling back to avoid censure. After the war Cornelia looked for the right opportunity.

She and other women of the era had a great deal to overcome, including women's long-engrained attitudes toward themselves. Throughout wars of the seventeenth, eighteenth, and early part of the nineteenth centuries, women who followed armies into battle were called "camp followers," which was the same as calling them prostitutes. Camp followers came from humble backgrounds, but they showed courage and patriotism, braved death and did what they could to relieve the suffering of wounded men. Armies did not systematically provide care for their sick or wounded until the Crimea.[259] In that war of 1854-6, Florence Nightingale introduced some concepts of modern nursing, revolutionized notions of a nurse's responsibilities and became an outspoken advocate for patients' needs. "It is often thought that medicine is the curative process," she wrote. "Surgery removes the bullet, but nature heals the wound." Nursing "is to put the patient in the best condition for nature to act upon him."[260] Nightingale insisted on hospital cleanliness. The dramatic decrease in the death rate she achieved provided a powerful example to those who followed.

Florence Nightingale also advised women how to handle social attitudes, telling them "to keep clear of both jargons now currently everywhere about the 'rights' of women, which urges women to do all that men do, merely because men do it,…and the other jargon, which urges women to do nothing men do…[and stick to] women's work…Surely a woman should bring the best she has, whatever that is, to the work of the world, without attending to either of those cries. Leave these jargons and go your way straight to work in simplicity and singleness of heart."[261] Under Nightingale's management the cleanliness, nutrition and ventilation of barracks hospitals improved. She returned to England a national hero and began a campaign to improve the quality of nursing in military hospitals.

However, disapproval about women working near battlefields persisted. The notion of "camp followers" lingered. Battlefields were dangerous, both physically and sexually. No respectable woman should serve.

The American Civil War cracked barriers, however, and offered women opportunities previously off limits. Women tested the boundaries of gender in their dealings with soldiers and coworkers. Some women flatly rejected restrictions based on sex. Other women had more traditional views and responded because they wanted to ease the suffering of wounded soldiers.

Whatever their reasons were to serve, four years of warfare allowed women like Cornelia to develop their talents—more than 18,200 women worked in Northern military hospitals as paid matrons, nurses, laundresses, and cooks. Their service eroded the popular idea that women's work ought to be strictly voluntary, an extension of caring for her family. Among the women who served as laundresses and cooks were 2,000 black women, many of them escaped slaves. Estimates are that another 2,000 women served in army hospitals as unpaid volunteers and independent operators like Clara Barton.[262] Many were assigned to drudgery in wards. They built fires, cooked, washed patients, irrigated festering wounds, cleaned slop from the floors, made beds and scrubbed undergarments. The title of "nurse" was given only to white women, even though cooks and cleaning women often performed the duties of nurses. Confederate women deserve equal credit for their efforts to alleviate suffering. Women serving on both sides had to prove their mettle daily. In sheer numbers alone—more than 20,000 all told—women hospital workers made an indispensable contribution.[263]

Wives, mothers, sisters, and daughters exchanged submissive roles for active ones, but not without resistance. Nowhere was this truer than in the medical corps and hospitals. At the outset of the Civil War, many of the men in charge had greeted female hospital workers with rabid opposition. Army surgeons wanted to keep female nurses out of the hospitals, but the government decided otherwise. Some men did their best to make life unbearable, trying to get women to leave. Female nurses quickly learned how difficult offering their services was going to be. Many did give up and go home. Only the strongest persevered against opposition. Their successes weakened the "gender" slavery of the previous eras. Like other women and men on the battlefields, Cornelia knew she was making history. She negotiated a hostile, male-dominated system and made gains.

In 1863 Linus Pierpont Brockett and Mary C. Vaughan began collecting information about women who distinguished themselves during the Civil War. They reported that women were reluctant to provide details about their service. In hindsight their resistance is understandable. The wisdom of pulling away from long-held notions of a woman's place was a hotly debated subject and one surrounded by confusion. Making public statements was too much to ask of many women. Privacy remained more important than recognition. Brockett and Vaughan found the way women withheld information frustrating; it prevented them from fully documenting all the ways women served.

The information they gathered was published in 1867: Women corresponded with auxiliary aid societies, accounted for goods, repacked and shipped them to where they were needed, sent out circulars appealing for aid. Women cared for thousands of sick and wounded as matrons of convalescent homes. Others devoted themselves to the freedom and education of former slaves as well as the welfare of poor whites. So many women supported the effort that the question for the authors became, not who should be named in an honor roll, but who could be omitted.[264]

When it came to Cornelia's contributions, Brockett and Vaughan had to rely on information provided by an agent of the Christian Commission. Here are some of the details they included about Cornelia. "Among the most zealous and untiring of the women who ministered to the wounded men 'at the front,' in the long and terrible campaign of the Army of the Potomac in 1864-5, was Miss Cornelia Hancock...[She] rendered efficient services at Gettysburg [starting in July 1863.] Of her work among the wounded men at Belle Plain and Fredericksburg, Mr. John Vassar, one of the most efficient agents of the Christian Commission, writes as follows:

> Miss Cornelia Hancock was the first lady who arrived at Fredericksburg to aid in the care of the wounded. As one of the many interesting episodes of the war, it has seemed that her good deeds should not be unheralded. She was also among the very first to arrive at Gettysburg after the fearful struggle, and for days and weeks ministered unceasingly to the suffering. During the past winter she remained constantly with the army in winter quarters, connecting herself with the Second Division of the Second Corps. So attached were the soldiers, and so grateful for her ministration in sickness, that they built a house for her, in which she remained until the general order for all to leave was given.

> … I well remember the mental ejaculation made when I saw her at such a time on the boat. I lost sight of her at Belle Plain, and had almost forgotten the circumstance, when, shortly before our arrival at Fredericksburg, she passed in an ambulance. On being assigned to a hospital of the Second Corps, I found she had preceded me, and was earnestly at work. It was no fictitious effort, but she had already prepared soup and farina, and was dispensing it to the crowds of poor fellows lying thickly about.

All day she worked, paying little attention to others, only assiduous in her sphere. When, the next morning, I opened a new hospital at the Methodist Church, I invited her to accompany me; she did so; and if success and amelioration of suffering attended the effort, it was in no small degree owing to her indefatigable labors. Within an hour from the time one hundred and twenty had been placed in the building, she had seen that good beef soup and coffee was administered to each.

…Were any dying, she sat by to soothe their last moments, to receive the dying message to friends at home, and when it was over to convey by letter the sad intelligence. Let me rise ever so early, she had already preceded me at work, and during the many long hours of the day, she never seemed to weary or flag; in the evening, when all in her own hospital had been fully cared for, she would go about the town with delicacies to administer to officers who were so situated they could not procure them. At night she sought a garret (and it was literally one) for her rest.

One can but feebly portray the ministrations of such a person. She belonged to no association—had no compensation. She commanded respect, for she was lady-like and well educated; so quiet and undemonstrative, that her presence was hardly noticed, except by the smiling faces of the wounded as she passed.

…Often would she make visits to the offices of the Sanitary and Christian Commissions, and when delicacies arrived, her men were among the first to taste them. Oranges, lemons, pickles, soft bread and butter, and even apple-sauce, were one or the other daily distributed. Such unwearied attention is the more appreciated, when one remembers the number of females who subsequently arrived, and the desultory and fitful labor performed. Passing from one hospital to another, and bestowing general sympathy, with small works, is not what wounded men want. It was very soon perceptible how the men in that hospital appreciated the solid worth of the one and the tinsel of the other.

This imperfect recognition is but a slight testimonial to the lady-like deportment and the untiring labors in behalf of sick and wounded soldiers of Miss Hancock."[265]

Only a few women wrote and published their own experiences. Women who publicized their accomplishments had to expect that someone would challenge their reputations. Praise in the press made a woman a target. Anonymous writers would ask editors to check on the woman's moral character. Louisa May Alcott, Jane Stuart Woolsey, Katharine Prescott Wormeley and a handful of others left accounts of wartime service. The rest chose to remain anonymous.

Cornelia's private papers also demonstrate how tenuous a woman's position was. Six months after the war ended, Frank Moore wrote to ask about her work for a book he was writing. Cornelia told him to ask her friends. She might be happy to be included but was wary of publicity.[266] If others wrote articles about Cornelia, she was savvy enough to let them.

A modern reader who picks up her letters has to wonder at her lack of self-promotion. She did not appear to have a personal agenda. Her goal was to serve the soldiers and freed slaves. Through her eyes one sees events without the biases of male valor, military campaigns, sectional pride or ego.

Throughout her life, Cornelia remained wary of publicity. The criticism she received while serving in field hospitals provided a strong incentive to stay out of the limelight. She wrote from City Point in June of 1864, "There never was a place where you have stronger friends or more violent enemies." It wasn't until many years later that she talked to family members about the range of her experiences and bequeathed her letters to Henrietta Stratton Jaquette, the granddaughter of a cousin.[267]

Whether touted in the press or not, women slipped into roles previously denied, filled a portion of the enormous need and earned new respect. They rethought their self-worth and accepted responsibility for things men said were outside of their control. The Civil War energized women. Even though military commands and society placed obstacles in their way, women achieved great things. They worked without social or psychological support. The bravest of them seized whatever chances opened up and provided starting points for future women to follow.[268] In the South, the war came to their doorsteps; battles in their towns and on their farms brought humanitarian work onto their front porches.

A new national identity started to emerge, even as each woman struggled to keep up with war's physical and emotional hardships. When they said goodbye to husbands and sons, brothers and lovers, many American women organized relief. Women's driving concern was the best methods to fill the gaps in government preparedness. They cooperated and conciliated men, demonstrated clarity of purpose, and were business-like and thorough about details. The Civil War and its aftermath created general social progress for men, and women advanced as well.[269] Like Cornelia, many learned on the job. Women's successes eroded entrenched views.

Modern women will sympathize with one of Cornelia's personal dilemmas—she fell in love with a man who didn't share her values. This was perhaps the hardest situation of all that Cornelia faced. While she was in Virginia, she served with Dr. Frederick Dudley, and he occupied many of her letters—too many to be just another physician. In one letter dated March 2, 1864, when she was age 24, she described Dudley as a young man of 22 years of age, who enlisted as a private but attained the rank of Major; a good surgeon; in constant motion; sharp-eyed and rather good looking.

She continually worries about him. "Dr. Dudley is perfectly reckless in time of battle. Dudley was caring for the wounded right on the front when he was shot."[270] She also knows the state of his health—at one point writing that he was sick and gone to bed. "Otherwise I should be in his house entertaining him." Another letter, written 10 days later, explained he pulled a tooth for Cornelia "with ease" and gave her a second picture of himself to replace one she had sent home for safe keeping.

Some passages Cornelia wrote about Dudley never made it into the printed version of her correspondence. When editing Cornelia's letters for publication in book form, Henrietta Stratton Jaquette left out lines where Cornelia expressed more than a friendly interest in Dr. Dudley. The reason Jaquette gave was respecting Cornelia's desire for privacy. Jacquette merely indicated Cornelia "never married. There is room, perhaps for speculation over a bundle of letters which were left, at her death, to be burned without reading. Her real interest in Dr. Frederick Dudley…is apparent, as is also his friendship for her."[271]

Letter dated June 9, 1864, in Cornelia's handwriting: "Dr. Dudley seemed glad to see me, the only trouble I have with him is he will go up on the breast works at the front for no other reason than to see, and some of these times he will be brought in dead or wounded."
Image Courtesy of Clements Library, University of Michigan

During the war Dudley visited the Hancock family while he was on leave, but Cornelia was unable to go along. Dudley's racist views on slavery caused great alarm among her family and friends, prompting a flurry of letters about his ideas and more concern than ever for Cornelia's way of living. After that, she confesses she would have been happier if he were an abolitionist. "Dr. Dudley had many good qualities," she wrote, "and I liked him very much. He amputated the limb of a poor black man and was concerned about him until he died. But to like a slave and do him justice does not exercise all parts of a Christian's character. My kind of humanity is to be able to love a white person equally well with the black."[272] In the same letter to her sister, Cornelia says she didn't doubt that Dr. Dudley's pro-slavery "proclivities" would bias the family against him.

Yet she made excuses for Dr. Dudley—something she did not do for others who failed to live up to her standards for equality. When her sister Ellen criticized him, Cornelia replied, [Ellen] "said she could not help letting his sins trouble her—his not being an abolitionist. I think that very foolish." Dr. Dudley "has done more towards crushing this rebellion than some of the ranting abolitionists."[273] Her defense also indicated she had given some thought to their future. Cornelia insisted that when he matured his opinions would change.

A letter she wrote on June 27, 1864, from City Point, Virginia, indicated he wanted her to transfer to his location and work with him. "Dr. Dudley has charge of the ambulance train now and will have the Div. hospital next winter and engaged me to come …but I tell him I will never leave Dr. Potter neither would I interfere with Mrs. Lee's prerogative." She went on to praise Dr. Dudley's care of soldiers: "He did more for the men than feed and clothe them. He discharged and furloughed them with more facility than anyone I ever saw handle red tape." When the army stationed him some six miles away, Cornelia worried that she would not see him again.

She continued to write about Dr. Dudley and express concern for him throughout the war. While Confederates held him prisoner, she wrote on December 15, 1864, "I received a letter from Dr. Dudley's mother; she thinks he is dead. I shall never think as if he never comes back. In fact I have seen as many that were with him, and they all say it is impossible that he can be dead." Her optimism at this point was a fervent hope rather than firsthand knowledge. When he was absent, she anticipated his return with "much rejoicing."[274]

Remembering her early childhood influences and Quaker sense of duty it becomes easier to see how the couple's differences became insurmountable. Marrying outside the Society of Friends was strongly discouraged, if not forbidden. Cornelia's own sense of the equality of the races provided another obstacle. Her desire to help former slaves remained strong while Dr. Dudley criticized her commitment to former slaves. She must have found insensitivity to suffering, based solely on skin color, hard to accept. Perhaps racial disagreement divided the couple as thoroughly as it divided the country.

What eventually happened between Dr. Dudley and Cornelia remains a mystery. Cornelia's biographer Jane T. McConnell says evidence suggests Cornelia met with Dr. Dudley in Alexandria before going home, but McConnell does not provide a source of that information. Even when talking to family members, Cornelia evaded the topic of when Dr. Dudley was going to visit after the war. McConnell claimed Dudley asked her to marry him, Cornelia turned him down, and Dudley waited six years for Cornelia to change her mind. Finally in 1871 he married another woman, named Sarah Jane Slocum. Eventually the Dudley's had three children.[275]

On December 15, 1864, Cornelia gave a clue about where her own ambitions would lead. "My mind is the principal part of me. I have very little physical." It is certain that Cornelia was in the habit of examining her life and carefully making choices. In that respect she was ahead of her time—her letters permit a strong sense of self to shine through. Her method of advancement was to make herself indispensable. If that didn't remove the obstacles, Cornelia simply did not take "no" for an answer.

It is known that she and Dr. Dudley remained on good terms. Years later when Cornelia applied for a government pension, the government bureau required her to prove she worked as a nurse for at least six months. A photocopy of the affidavit, attesting to her length of service in the Salem County Historical Society files, showed

Dr. Frederick Dudley signed the paperwork. According to Historical Society records,[276] Cornelia applied for and received a government pension from 1895 to 1927.

The pain of returning to a postwar world was not often discussed—by soldiers, nurses or society. Cornelia's story is one of incremental progress. She took the first step and developed a better understanding of her own potential. Then she continued to ignore "the common herd."

Her memory for the struggles of slaves was better than most people's—and it motivated her to do something to help. She faced and made a decision not to return to a quiet lifestyle but to continue, as her conscience dictated, to do the "duty that lies nearest." She had walked onto the Gettysburg battlefield and suppressed the urge to turn and run, as stretcher bearers and ambulance drivers had. People at home disapproved. They called her a reprobate and condemned her lifestyle, but she worked through all the obstacles. She and other female workers shared the soldiers' fearful fatigue and pains of hunger—and shared a collective experience that redefined America. For Cornelia the heady experience of saving lives and improving horrible conditions must have become addictive.

Toward the end of the war, she offered an incident typical of her self-assurance. In this instance, a soldier was desperate to go home for his wife's funeral. Leave of absences were rare and difficult to obtain. Enlisted men were granted leave at the superior's discretion by a commander actually quartered with the soldier's company or regiment. Weapons and accoutrements remained behind, and furlough papers gave a detailed description of each soldier's physical appearance, return and departure dates, unit designation, pay and subsistence allowances.[277] Red tape did not stop Cornelia. She went directly to Grant's Adjutant General. The result was: "My fame has spread the length and breadth of this camp. Such a miracle [securing a furlough] accomplished in so short a time. All who know me say it is easier to grant my request than to undertake to deny me because I am so persevering."[278]

Reconstruction

The Civil War pitted brother against brother—and created deep-seated hatred. Reconstruction was an era of unprecedented political conflict and far-reaching changes. The national debate centered on three questions: On what terms should the Confederacy rejoin the Union? Who should establish these terms, Congress or the President? What should be the place of the former slaves in the political life of the South?[279] With such monumental decisions looming, the role of women received less attention and support than it should have.

As long as what women intended to do outside the home was similar to their roles inside it, they were accepted. Society believed men and women, by nature, were meant to occupy separate spheres. Many women relief workers moved into teaching and social work because those jobs did not overturn prewar roles of helping others. Women had learned to manipulate the system, but were allowed to do so primarily to aid suffering soldiers. The carnage of war ended, but social injustice remained.

Experience and new skills did not translate into opportunities for women. Dire conditions confronted women in the South. Many now needed to work, but the stigma attached to work had not lifted. Hospital duty had provided women, North and South, with training in teamwork, management of resources and distribution. Cornelia learned these skills well. Still, few people wanted to dismantle the traditional role for women. Gender was a source of conflict, as was race and sectional animosity between northerners and southerners. On September 11, 1865, Dorthea Dix received a short note, abolishing the Women's Nursing Bureau and discharging all female nurses.

Women needed to find additional resolve if they were going to move forward. Vesta Swarts, another nurse, went on to become a physician. Courage and imagination smoldered inside them, but only a few managed to attain new roles.

When soldiers no longer needed her, Cornelia could have slipped quietly back into peacetime society. She tried going home but could no longer live a rural existence. Her "keen sense of the needs of the often helpless" African Americans plagued her.[280]

Connections made through Dr. and Ellen Child helped her understand the dangers of Reconstruction. The pitiful conditions she witnessed in 1863 at the contraband hospital in Washington still haunted her. As early as February of 1866, Cornelia understood government would not live up to martyred President Lincoln's goal of healing the nation's wounds. She wrote: "I satisfied myself there was no hope for the colored people through him [President Johnson and the administration.]"[281]

The time Cornelia spent among former slaves convinced her of the vital need for education. She knew instruction provided the best way to improve their situations. Their plight became the next battlefront. For her, the war had been necessary to do away with the horrors of slavery. The horrendous sacrifice flowed into an urgent need to build a better life for those who had been held in bondage.

She shifted from the role of nurse to that of teacher. With help from the Philadelphia Quaker Society of Friends and Laura Towne, she made plans to travel south and start a school. Before leaving, however, Cornelia explained her decision to her mother this way: "I do not want you to give yourself any concern about my going so far as I am just as well off one place as another and if I should die I shall be just as ready as a few years from now. I amused our children [her sister Ellen's] last evening making my will. I left to Sallie my medal. To Eddie my chain and trinkets," and so on.[282]

After she and Laura Towne arrived in South Carolina, Cornelia learned how difficult teaching former slaves would be. Southerners mourned their lost cause.[k] The South began to memorialize the attempt to maintain states' rights. In January 1866 Cornelia said Charleston-area residents "seem to take delight in torturing the feelings of the negro in every way they can so as to escape the penalty of law. Take from the negro the protection of such men as Gen. Saxton and the good men of the Freedman's Bureau and you will

---

[k] The "Lost Cause," the title of Edward A. Pollard's 1866 history of the Confederacy, first referred to the defeat, but in time it also came to mean how the South remembered the war.

have inaugurated as near an approach to slavery as it is possible."[283] She wrote that ominous passage on the day the government announced Major General Rufus Saxton would be replaced.[284] Saxton had been serving as an assistant commissioner for the Freedmen's Bureau, and he had pursued a policy of settling freed slaves onto land confiscated from white landowners. By the end of 1865 only 152,000 Union soldiers remained in the South.[285]

She found South Carolina to be "The most forlorn country I have ever seen …They have the subject of reconstruction before their mind…the people said every kind of disagreeable thing in our hearing but would not condescend to speak to the Yankee[s]….They really look starved in their faces…I expect soon all teachers shall be driven off but we shall not go easily."[286]

Miss Towne was impressed with Cornelia's resourcefulness and sent her off on her own. Across Charleston harbor in Mount Pleasant, South Carolina, Cornelia discovered a Presbyterian Church, riddled with bullets. The sun shown through holes in the roof, but when she sat down on the steps, children gathered around her. She asked if the children would like to have a school, and the answer was uniformly 'yes.'

Cornelia told them to come back in two days and made a promise to open a school "without much knowledge of conditions, and the next move was to find the authority existing to make life safe, and I found it to consist of a United States Provost-Marshal….I made arrangements to come over from Charleston and open the school as I had promised the children I would do—and on arriving found fifty children awaiting me."[287] She moved into the "Secesh" village in January of 1866, where the monumental conflict of Reconstruction took its toll.

Poverty meant something different from what it did back home in New Jersey. "It means destitution that forbids any hope of anything better. Stealing on account of extreme poverty is the order of the day."[288] Soldiers of both armies had plundered the countryside; the residents needed everything from a dress to a pot to cook hominy. Cornelia quickly found out how exasperating it was to go through the Freedman's Bureau for aid, but she had no choice. She had to be conciliatory. If she did not hide her anger, African American residents could lose desperately needed help. "I wish all your children [her sister Ellen's family] could see the little bundles of rags that come to school."[289]

After the school had been open for a while, Cornelia had 150 scholars, who "are more interested [than the ones I taught in the North] and decidedly smarter. I am blessed with all that makes one place more desirable to me than another. ...I feel it a great privilege to be...situated in the midst of people so very needy in...everything that makes life endurable."[290] She found the students "in no way more trouble" than white children except that they were more excitable and laughed more easily. When given books, the children treasured their primers and held them tightly.

After classes ended for the day, Cornelia walked to a few adjoining plantations to visit people in need of rations. She wrote about one elderly couple. The man was nearly 100 years old, and his frail wife had been physically beaten by a life of hard labor. Cornelia asked about their children and was told the woman had given birth to ten, but nine had been sold and were lost to her. When asked how they lived, the woman showed the ground she had prepared to plant a crop. Cornelia then remarked about their threadbare bedding, asking how they got through cold nights. "The woman said they did not dare to go to bed at all for fear they would freeze, but sat up in the fireplace all night." The couple deliberately ate while she was there, and thanked God devoutly for a few grits and the head of a coon. Through the Bureau of Freedman, Cornelia helped them receive government blankets and rations, causing the old woman to thank God for sending her "one good Missus" before she died.[291]

Cornelia understood the animosity Reconstruction generated and acknowledged the risks she was taking. "We shall all leave when the military does. The Rebels would tar and feather us and go unpunished."[292] When she looked past individual acts of charity to Reconstruction as a whole, Cornelia despaired. In February 1866 she wrote "The Freedman's Bureau seem as a class to dislike to help the blacks. But it is through them alone that we can get efficient aid, so I feel it worthwhile to conciliate rather than exasperate."[293] From her position among the destitute, she decided there was no hope to ease the troubles of former slaves. "In…[land] questions much depends on the person who interprets the titles—pro-Rebel or desirous of helping struggling humanity."[294] If it weren't for seafood readily available along the coast and the willingness of former slaves to work, people would have starved. She envisioned there would never be any justice for Freedmen except if it was enforced by Federal bayonets.[295]

General George G. Meade offered a different perspective on the role of federal authority during Reconstruction. After the war Meade commanded the Third Military District, covering Georgia, Alabama and Florida. He arrived in Atlanta on January 5, 1868. Constitutional conventions in these states suffered from fraud, lack of finances and endless political bickering. Meade convened a board of officers to investigate the charges of fraudulent districting and registration; the board proved none of the charges. As a result, Meade "interfered" and proposed compromises. When the three states were finally admitted to and represented in Congress, Meade immediately issued orders declaring a cessation to all military intervention in civil affairs. His eagerness to return authority to locals—still wrangling over power—was evident in his report, "The inauguration of civil government was to me, personally, a source of great relief, charged as I had been with almost unlimited powers."[296]

On the whole, Union soldiers had not enlisted to destroy slavery or defend black rights. Military duty during Reconstruction, to them, had nothing to do with preserving the nation or protecting their families.[297] Both sides had defended their idea of what society should be. Both fought enemies that were savage. Both sides discovered savagery in themselves. After the war the North turned away from its responsibilities; the South sought to recapture their past way of life.[298] Most northern soldiers had signed on to rescue the Union—nothing more. Men at arms had maintained "liberty." Now they showed little interest in dwelling on postwar realities. Rather than come to terms with still smoldering hatreds, northern writers portrayed the fighting nobly as a national redemption. Pageantry replaced grizzly suffering. The bloody, confused ending turned into self-congratulation.[299] Both sides created myths about their role in mass destruction.[300]

Rather than deal with sectional divisions, the suffering caused by the war, or the plight of slaves, northerners dubbed the conflict as exalted. A nation had redeemed itself; general amnesia began to block out the bloody triumph. The shock of combat and discouragement of Reconstruction got buried below the surface. Bloodshed and racism was described as "the late unpleasantness."[301]

It is certain that Cornelia was lonely and worried in South Carolina—yet the overall tone of her letters is one of satisfaction. Working with children was her way of making the war count for something. She replaced loss with purpose. When a northern visitor asked her students what he should tell the people who supported the school, a girl about twelve years old stood up and said in a loud voice, "Tell them I thank them for sending our kind teachers, our boxes of clothing and the books from which we learn our lessons."[302] With responses like that, it felt providence had sent Cornelia to the right place.[303]

The Philadelphia Friends Association for the Aid and Elevation of Freemen continued to support the classes. The school became the Laing School. In 1868 the Freedmen's Bureau paid the rent for a brick mansion, large enough to accommodate the school and house the teachers. The Laing School became a pioneer among southern schools. In January 1868 Cornelia summarized her efforts. "Surely great changes have taken place with these children. No one ought to feel discouraged...although they have yet no elevating or educating *home* influences, which will, of course, operate much against them in this generation. They have the lessons of extreme poverty and much oppression yet to suffer. The depressed state of business in the South makes it very hard for them to get employment at remunerative rates; and the dense ignorance existing in the grown people's minds makes it extremely difficult. I consider the *schools* have been the only systematic agency for permanent good."[304]

For 10 years, until 1875, Cornelia remained in South Carolina as the school's principal. At that time poor health forced her to give up her duties in the South and return to Philadelphia. The Laing school continues its work, exists under the same name, but in modern times as a part of the public school system.

In the 1870's, Philadelphia was a city of nearly one million people. It was the country's third largest city and home to the country's second biggest port,[305] but a series of economic setbacks rocked the city and the nation: a Black Friday panic of 1869, the outbreak of influenza in 1872, and in 1873 the perception United States monetary policy was unstable with regard to silver. One of the Philadelphia banks contributed to a financial panic that spread around the globe. Jay Cooke & Company had been pooling railroad securities and selling them to other financial institutions. According to the bank managers, railways were a good, stable source of income, but in the 1870s it became apparent the claims were too good to be true. September 1873 Jay Cooke & Company went bankrupt. The stock market and the securities of other financial organizations plummeted. Hundreds of institutions failed. Credit flow came to a stop; an additional 60 trading companies and 90 railway companies went under. Unemployment ran up to twenty-five percent.[306] The depression in the United States and Europe lasted until 1879.

Cornelia began to work in Philadelphia in 1878 for the Society for Organizing Charity.[1] Here she advocated for the poor and served as Superintendent. In that role, Cornelia received the names of all those who applied for aid, sent applicants who lived in other wards to the proper agency, and then entered the names and local residents in an "Inquiry Book." One annual report shows they had 540 applicants, and of these 281 were entered in their registry. The report also indicates the Superintendent and an independent visitor called on every applicant at their homes to make sure individuals truly needed help.

Many families were plagued by alcoholism. Even when parents abused alcohol, the Society tried to help care for children. If they provided shoes and clothing for the children, it was on the condition they attended school. The motto quoted in their report is: Charity's eyes must be open as well as her hands.

After becoming acquainted with the applicants, they were able to assess need, encourage and assist families. The Society asked the public not to give handouts to those who begged on the streets,

---

[1] Later known as the Family Society of Philadelphia.

stating street beggars were often impostors. Instead they offered transportation tickets to send applicants to their office, where cases could be investigated before relief was given.[307]

Cornelia became one of the first social workers. She believed that a woman, who gave fully of her time, intelligence and energy, should not only be concerned with direct help to the needy but also with organizing others. When others had the means to help but no idea how to begin, she helped them learn the best ways to structure aid. Her contact with the poorest families convinced her that children in particular needed assistance. In 1882 she helped found the Children's Aid of Pennsylvania and served on the committee that hired the first paid social worker. The goals she espoused were to help suffering children in ways that lifted them out of poverty and gave them a chance to succeed later in life. As Secretary to the Board of Directors, she wrote that inquiry had to "enlighten" charity to ensure results.[308]

The final chapter in Cornelia's service career began in 1884 with a move to Wrightsville, a squalid, isolated settlement of 40 shanty houses in south Philadelphia. Cornelia's friend Edith Wright leased the site from absentee owners among them Edith's father Peter, a wealthy ship owner. The two women set about to duplicate a successful social experiment from England. They wanted to demonstrate that enlightened management of slum properties led to reform—as well as financial gain. The residents of Wrightsville were primarily immigrants, employed by nearby refineries. Edith and Cornelia made rules for the residents but also kept the property repaired and secured missing municipal services.[309] Hancock and Wright enforced their rules of cleanliness and order. They pressured city bureaus for paved streets and police protection, placed an effective principal in the school and opened a public library with books in both English and German. By 1914 all the residents of Wrightsville were homeowners—a triumphal outcome.[310] Cornelia continued community work until 1914 and then retired.

Cornelia had gone off to war, risked death, her health and reputation to become a field nurse. She received no government training and had no expectation she would get paid. Her only qualifications were a lack of hesitation and fervent desire to meet every challenge. She did not directly confront the limits nineteenth century society placed on women. At the same time, she refused to let anyone stop her from assuming a useful, public role. The letters she wrote provide a unique account of the bloodiest conflict in the nation's history and the shame of Reconstruction.

People who live through horrendous events wonder how they survive when many others perish. They struggle to put the physical and psychological terror into words, but often fall short. Personal accounts from the American Civil War show how difficult it was to survive—and to describe the human carnage. In May and June of 1862, for example, hospital boats at White House Landing, Virginia, evacuated 11,000 wounded from Fair Oaks and Seven Days' battles. When 4,500 sick and wounded started arriving from Fair Oaks, only five surgeons were on duty. Many soldiers had traveled three days without surgical attention or food.[311] Sophronis Bucklin, American Civil War nurse, wrote, "The sight which presented itself baffles every effort at correct description."[312] Cornelia struggled to express her grief too. At times, sarcasm helped put the sights into words. "One of my favorite resorts is our dead house, some such fine looking men die."[313]

Two incidents help to describe her legacy. Twenty years after the Civil War ended she attended a Grand Army of the Republic encampment. A veteran came into the Army Nurse Association and asked if Miss Hancock was there. She moved to greet the man, who asked if she could remember the church hospital in Fredericksburg. The hospital was easy to recall but not one man out of the great number treated, so he refreshed Cornelia's memory. The doctors passed by because he was too severely injured to spend time on, but Cornelia came by with a colored woman and washed him and put on a clean shirt. When the doctors came around again, they had him moved into the church where she fed him with soft food because it was difficult for him to swallow. He recovered and, as a token of appreciation, had a medal made, inscribed with two of the battles Cornelia helped him.

The second incident concerns Captain Dod, who described the kindness Cornelia showed him in a letter[314] to his mother, "I came here day before yesterday, was so much under the influence of opium and quinine and suffering so much pain that I could not write....Without my knowing it she solicited permission from Dr. Hammond to let me take my meals with her. At every meal she send an orderly who when I am well enough carries me down."[315] Cornelia did the best she could but on August 27, 1864, wrote, "Capt. Dod is now dying in my bed....His mother came last night. It is a deathbed just like a home deathbed and is very affecting."[316] At the same time Cornelia nursed Captain Dod, there were 2,200 men in the hospital. He was one of many—yet she gave him the kind of devoted attention usually reserved for family. Because of this gentle care, Captain Dod said Cornelia was as much loved as Florence Nightingale was in the British Army. A note dated April 25, 1892, from Dod's brother, who was President of The First National Bank of Hoboken, New Jersey, informed Cornelia that their mother had left Cornelia a small legacy for her "great kindness."

Near the end of her life Cornelia went to live with a niece in Atlantic City, where she died at the age of 87. No formal monument was created to honor Cornelia's lifework. Her grave marker is a flat stepping stone in the yard of the Quaker Meeting House in Hancock's Bridge, New Jersey. The simple setting cannot compete with the great events of her lifetime, but the beauty of the tall trees and nearby marsh provide a well deserved resting place. Considering her caution about publicity, an obscure plaque appears to be the recognition she might have chosen for herself.

A lifetime of devotion is the real monument. Her accomplishments reverberate across the decades. Without any expectations of power or influence, she and her contemporaries reshaped America. Single-mindedness of purpose made it possible for America to rescue its founding principles. Despite ruthless conditions, Cornelia eased the suffering of others. Although she choked on injustice, she suppressed her rage and substituted gentle persuasion to secure clothing, food, and education for those in need.

She was not dissuaded by the enormity of the task but enlisted support from others and eased hardships of the poor.

Cornelia's perspective was a moral one. Her parents, and the Quaker Society of Friends they belong to, instilled early childhood lessons on equality of the races and submission to God's will. These early influences remained strong throughout her life. Beliefs about proper conduct influenced Cornelia's thoughts, words and actions— even when confronted with the carnage of war. She witnessed some of the war's greatest events and wrote about them with compassion, a sense of cooperation, forgiveness, and modesty.

The Civil War was the end of innocence for states, physicians and society. The nation as a whole turned away from incomprehensible destruction. Only men and women with rare values, such as Cornelia, put themselves on the frontlines in the ongoing battle for freedom. Values shaped Cornelia for service—and service like hers shaped the nation.

Appendix I

Organization of Civil War Field Armies[317]

Armies were the largest operational organizations. Union forces followed a general policy of naming their armies for the rivers near which they operated. The Confederates named their armies from the states or regions in which they were active. The Union had an Army of the Tennessee, not to be confused with the Confederate Army of Tennessee. There were at least 16 armies on the Union side and 23 on the Confederate side. Field armies were divided into the following units:

Unit	Approximate Size	Usual Commander
Company	100 men	Captain
Regiment	1,000 men	Colonel
Brigade	4,000 men	Brigadier General
Division	12,000 men	Major General
Corps	2 to 4 divisions	Major General

Acknowledgements

The staff at Hancock House in southern New Jersey, under the direction of Jean Powell, does more than watch over the ancestral Hancock home. Their colorful story about a massacre there during the American Revolution is enough to pique anyone's curiosity. Apparently an early caretaker of the building spilled chicken blood in the attic to "flesh" out details no one has been able to document. The docent of Hancock House clarified points about the family's history available on the Internet and other sources. The staff also made sure I stopped at the Salem County Historical Society where Librarian Beverly Stanley offered their records and photos. The guidance given at both institutions made it possible to understand Cornelia's place in history.

Touring the museum and grounds of Gettysburg National Park brought the grand scale of Civil War events into focus. I highly recommend military historian Wayne Motts' audio tour recording about the Battle of Gettysburg. It provides a wealth of information in ways a novice can understand. His talk allowed me to understand the logistics and the human toll of the Civil War's bloodiest battle.

I am also indebted to Janet Bloom at William L. Clements Library, University of Michigan, in Ann Arbor. She made microfilm of Cornelia Hancock's letters from the Library's collection available. Henrietta Stratton Jaquette, the granddaughter of a cousin, published Cornelia's letters in book form in 1937, but Jaquette edited out even more. The microfilm showed what was left out at publication—mostly personal passages about Cornelia's interactions with a handsome, young doctor named Fred Dudley. Jaquette writes that Cornelia wanted her relationship with Dr. Dudley to remain private. Viewing the original documents showed that, even though Cornelia was trying to protect the people back home from what went on at the front, at times Cornelia could not help letting the urgency and peril of war, and her affection for Dr. Dudley slip in.

I must also acknowledge the helpful opinions of fellow writers C. Michael Becker and Dennis Leuchtenburg, who read the first draft and suggested ways to improve the manuscript. Vickie Speek gave wonderful editorial assistance and helped polish the working version. Their comments were invaluable; I hope I used their suggestions to good advantage. Cornelia Hancock's story deserves the best treatment I can possibly give. After a while, it felt right for me to write about "Cornelia" with no title or surname. After you read her story, I hope you are on a first name basis with her too.

Georgiann Baldino, February 21, 2010

Select Bibliography

Adams, George Worthington, Doctors in Blue, *The Medical History of the Union Army in the Civil War*, Henry Schuman, (New York, 1952).

Bollet, Alfred Jay, M.D., *Civil War Medicine Challenges and Triumphs,* Galen Press, (Tucson, 2002).

Bucklin, Sophronia E., *Hospital and Camp,* John E. Potter and Company, (Philadelphia, 1869).

Burstyn, Joan N., Editor-in-chief, *Women's Project of New Jersey, Past and promise: lives of New Jersey women*, Scarecrow Press, Inc., (Metuchen, 1990).

Freeman, Frank R., *Gangrene and Glory, Medical Care during the American Civil War,* Associated University Presses, Inc., (New York, 1998).

Hancock, Cornelia, Correspondence and papers, Microfilm provided by Clements Library, University of Michigan.

Jaquette, Henrietta Stratton, Editor, *Letters of Cornelia Hancock: South after Gettysburg,* Thomas Y. Crowell, (New York, 1937).

Meade, George G., *The life and letters of George Gordon Meade: major-general United States Army,* Vol. 2 Charles Scribner's Sons, (New York, 1913).

McConnell, Jane T., *Cornelia, the Story of a Civil War Nurse,* Thomas Y. Crowell Company, (Binghamton, 1959).

McConnell, Stuart Charles, *Glorious contentment: the Grand Army of the Republic,* University of North Carolina Press, (Chapel Hill, 1992).

Motts, Wayne, Recorded Audio Tour, *Gettysburg Field Guide,* Travel Brains, Inc. 2008.

Mitchell, Reid, *Civil War Soldiers,* Viking Adult, (New York, 1988).

Nighttingale, Florence, *Notes on Nursing,* Dover Publications, (New York, 1969).

Oates, Stephen B., *Clara Barton, Woman of Valor,* Free Press, (New York, 1994).

Rutkow, Ira M., *Bleeding Blue and Gray: Civil War surgery and the evolution of American Medicine,* Random House, (New York, 2005).

Salem County Historical Society, 79-83 Market Street, Salem, NJ., Library archival files 2009, various articles and papers including Pension Affidavit.

Schultz, Jane E., *Women at the Front, Hospital Workers in Civil War America,* University of North Carolina Press, (Chapel Hill, 2004).

Wiley, Bell Irvin, *The Life of Billy Yank, The Common Soldier of the Union*, Louisiana State University Press, (Baton Rouge, 1998).

Endnotes

[1] Henrietta Stratton Jaquette, Ed., *South After Gettysburg, Letters of Cornelia Hancock, 1863-1868*, Thomas Y. Crowell Company (New York, 1956), p. 100.

[2] Kevin O'Beirne, "June 3, 1864: Irish Regiments Fight for Grant at Cold Harbor," http://www.thewildgeese.com/pages/coldharb.html, May 30, 1864.

[3] Jaquette, p. 27.

[4] Jane E. Schultz, Women at the Front, Hospital Workers in Civil War America, University of North Carolina Press, (Chapel Hill, 2004), p. 179.

[5] Jaquette, p. 3

[6] Joan N. Burstyn, Editor-in-chief, *Women's Project of New Jersey, Past and promise: lives of New Jersey women*, Scarecrow Press, Inc., (Metuchen, 1990), p. 70.

[7] Jane T. McConnell, *Cornelia, the Story of a Civil War Nurse*, Thomas Y. Crowell Company, (Binghamton, 1959), pp. 6, 16.

[8] Jane McConnell, p. 151.

[9] Jaquette, p. 3-4.

[10] Jane McConnell, p. 9 and 32.

[11] Alfred Jay Bollet, M.D., *Civil War Medicine Challenges and Triumphs*, Galen Press, (Tucson, 2002), p 2 and 76.

[12] Jane McConnell, 9.

[13] Neil Kagan, Editor, and Stephen G. Hyslop, Author, *Eyewitness to the Civil War*, National Geographic Society, (Washington, D.C., 2006,) p. 184.

[14] Linus Pierpont Brockett and Mary C. Vaughan, *Woman's Work in the Civil War: A Record of Heroism, Patriotism, and Patience*, Project Gutenberg EBook, Zeigler, McCurdy & Co., 1867, p. 62.

[15] Bollet, p. 410.

[16] Schultz, p. 96.

[17] Viney, W. & Zorich, S. (1982). Contributions to the history of psychology XXIX: Dorothea Dix. Psychological Reports, 50, 211-218.

[18] Ira M. Rutkow, *Bleeding Blue and Gray: Civil War surgery and the evolution of American Medicine,* Random House, (New York, 2005), p. 171.

[19] *Civil War Nurse, The Diary and Letters of Hannah Ropes*, Introduction and commentary by John R. Brumgardt, http://www.civilwarhome.com/civilwarnurses.htm, June 30, 2009.

[20] Bollet, p. 410.

[21] Schultz, p. 20.

[22] *Civil War Nurse, The Diary and Letters of Hannah Ropes*, Introduction and commentary by John R. Brumgardt, The University of Tennessee Press, (Knoxville, 1980).

23 Stephen B. Oates, *Clara Barton, Woman of Valor*, Free Press, (New York, 1994), p. 374.

24 Jaquette, p. 76-7.

25 Jaquette, p. 145

26 Jaquette, p. 76

27 Jaquette, p. 17

28 Bollet, p. 410.

29 William A. Hammond to Abraham Lincoln, Wednesday, July 16, 1862 (Catholic and Protestant nurses) Abraham Lincoln Papers at the Library of Congress. Transcribed and Annotated by the Lincoln Studies Center, Knox College. Galesburg, Illinois.

30 Jaquette, p. 131.

31 Jaquette, p. 18.

32 Jaquette, p. 3-5.

33 Jaquette, p. 5-6.

34 Oates, p. 376.

35 Schultz, p. 97.

36 Harold Elk Straubing, In Hospital and Camp, Stackpole Books, (Mechanicsburg, 1993), p. 55-6.

37 Bollet, p. 405.

38 Bollet, p. 405.

39 Jaquette, p. 11.

40 Jaquette, p. 85.

41 Schultz, p. 97.

42 Jaquette, p. 134.

43 Jaquette, p. 123.

44 Schultz, p. 90-1.

45 Schultz, p. 19.

46 Drew Gilpin Faust, *This Republic of Suffering, Death and the American Civil War*, Alfred A. Knopf, (New York, 2008), p. 10

47 Jaquette, p. 53.

48 Straubing, p. 99-100.

49 Jaquette, p. 17

50 Bollet, p. 13.

51 Civil War Medicine Page, www.civilwarhome.com/civilwarmedicineintro.htm Article by Edward L. Musnson, M.D. Major, Medical Department, United States Army, June 30, 2009.

52 "The Medical and Surgical History of the War of the Rebellion." (1861-65.) Part III, Volume II, Chapter XIV—The Medical Staff and Materia Chirugica.

53 Bollet, p. 218.

54 Rutkow, p. 25.

55 Bollet, p. 219.

[56] Freemon, p. 107

[57] Jaquette, p. 123.

[58] Bollet, p. 3.

[59] Bollet, p. 16.

[60] Bollet, p. 2.

[61] Mitchell, p. 62.

[62] Bollet, p. 105.

[63] Bell Irvin Wiley, *The Life of Billy Yank, The Common Soldier of the Union*, Louisiana State University Press, (Baton Rouge, 1998), p. 144.

[64] Frank R. Freeman, *Gangrene and Glory, Medical Care during the American Civil War*, Associated University Presses, Inc., (New York, 1998), p. 36.

[65] From the Official Records: GENERAL ORDERS No. 147 Regulations for the organization of the ambulance corps and the management of ambulance trains GENERAL ORDERS No. 106 Public 22 - An Act of Congress to establish a uniform system of ambulances in the armies of the United States Source(s): The National Historical Society's "The Image of War, Volume IV, Fighting For Time" and "The Official Records of the War of the Rebellion."

[66] Jaquette, p. 17.

[67] Jaquette, p. 104.

[68] Bollet, p. 52.

[69] Jaquette, p. 77.

[70] Jaquette, p. 35.

[71] Jaquette, p. 59.

[72] Professor T. Longmore, *Treatise on the Transport of Sick and Wounded Troops*, London, 1869, p. 292.

[73] Bollet, p. 104-5.

[74] Rutkow, p. 143-5.

[75] Rutkow, p. 183.

[76] Rutkow, p. 275.

[77] Jaquette, p. 13.

[78] Freemon, p. 36.

[79] Wiley, p. 130.

[80] Bollet, p. 226.

[81] Holland Thompson, *The Photographic History of the Civil War,* The Civil War Medicine Page, http://www.civilwarhome.com/sanitarycommission.htm, May 11, 2010.

[82] Schultz, p. 13.

[83] Wilson Small, "The Sanitary Commission To The Rescue," 5 June, 1862. http://www.civilwarhome.com/sanitarycommtorescue.htm, June 30, 2009.

[84] Rutkow, p. 80.

[85] Rutkow, p. 79.

[86] Jaquette, p. 37.

[87] Bollet, p. 243.

[88] Bollet, p. 235-6.

[89] Bollet, p. 248.

[90] Rutkow, p. 123.

[91] Bollet, p. 189-90.

[92] Rutkow, p. 151.

[93] Rutkow, p. 4.

[94] Rutkow, p. 4.

[95] Jaquette, p. 74.

[96] Meade, p. 7.

[97] George G. Meade, *The life and letters of George Gordon Meade: major-general United States Army,* Vol. 2 Charles Scribner's Sons, (New York, 1913), p.16.

[98] Meade, p. 15.

[99] Bollet, p. 243.

[100] Bollet, p. 125.

[101] Freemon, p. 111.

[102] *The Patriot Daughters of Lancaster, Hospital Scenes After the Battle of Gettysburg,* http://library.thinkquest.org/17525/aftermath.htm, June 24, 2009.

[103] Jaquette, p. 7

[104] Jonathan Letterman, U.S. Army, Medical Director, Army of the Potomac, O.R. Series I, Volume XXVVII/I Gettysburg Campaign.

[105] National Park Service, Gettysburg National Military Park, http://www.nps.gov/gett/historyculture/index.htm, June 24, 2009.

[106] Bollet, p. 396.

[107] Freemon, p. 124.

[108] Jaquette, 6.

[109] Drew Gilpin Faust, *This Republic of Suffering: Death and the American Civil War,* Alfred A. Knopf, (New York, 2008,) p. 102, 102 & 213

[110] Jonathan Letterman, U.S. Army, Medical Director, Army of the Potomac, O.R. Series I, Volume XXVVII/I Gettysburg Campaign.

[111] Freemon, p. 112-114.

[112] Jaquette, p. 12.

[113] Jaquette, p. 71.

[114] Jaquette, p. 17.

[115] Meade, p. 110-114.

[116] Meade, p. 132.

[117] Meade, p. 134.

[118] William E. Barton, *The Life of Abraham Lincoln,* Books, Inc. (Boston, 1943,) p175-184.

[119] Goodwin, p. 532.

[120] Wiley, p. 132.

[121] Bollet, p. 54.

[122] Jaquette, p. 13.

[123] Report of Surg. Jonathan Letterman, U.S. Army, Medical Director, Army of the Potomac. O.R—SERIES I—VOLUME XXVII/1 [S# 43] — Gettysburg Campaign.

[124] Bancroft and Dunning, Eds., *The Reminiscences of Carl Schurz*, The Reminiscences Of Carl Schurz, Vol II, Internet Archive, Akce Universal Digital Library, Numeric_id: 70154, Public_date: 2003-09-23 10:14:01.

[125] Jaquette, p. 10-11.

[126] Jaquette, p. 11

[127] Jaquette, p. 14.

[128] 1st Minnesota Infantry Monument, http://www.findagrave.com/cgi-bin/fg.cgi?page=gr&GRid=6935558, June 30, 2009.

[129] Bollet, p. 125.

[130] Wiley, p. 128-9.

[131] Bollet, p. 199-200.

[132] "Some of the Wonders of Modern Surgery," *The Atlantic Monthly*, Volume 21, Issue 125, March 1868.

[133] "The Medical and Surgical History of the War of the Rebellion. (1861-65.) --Part III, Volume II, Chapter XIII. Anaesthetics," Civil War Medicine Page, http://www.civilwarhome.com/civilwarmedicine.htm, April 27, 2010.

[134] "The Medical and Surgical History of the War of the Rebellion. (1861-65.) --Part III, Volume II, Chapter XIII. Anaesthetics," Civil War Medicine Page, http://www.civilwarhome.com/civilwarmedicine.htm, April 27, 2010

[135] CASE 1250, The Civil War Medicine Page, http://www.civilwarhome.com/civilwarmedicineintro.htm, June 30, 2009.

[136] Jaquette, p. 19.

[137] "The Medical and Surgical History of the War of the Rebellion. (1861-65.) --Part III, Volume II, Chapter XIII. Anaesthetics," Civil War Medicine Page, http://www.civilwarhome.com/civilwarmedicine.htm, April 27, 2010.

[138] Sophronia Bucklin, *In Hospital and Camp,* John E. Potter and Company, 1869, p. 270.

[139] John R. Brumgardt, Editor, *Civil War Nurse, the Diary and Letters of Hannah Ropes,* The University of Tennessee Press, (Knoxville, 1980), p.57.

[140] Rutkow, p. 234-5.

[141] Bollet, p. 212-3.

[142] Bollet, p. 199.

[143] Civil War Medicine Page, http://www.civilwarhome.com/civilwarmedicine.htm, The Civil War Society's "Encyclopedia of the Civil War," April 27, 2010.

[144] Jaquette, p. 16.

[145] Faust, p. 6 & 233

[146] Bucklin, p. 291.

[147] Jaquette, p. 95.

[148] Jane McConnell, p. 96.

[149] Jaquette, p. 19.

[150] Jaquette, p. 68.

[151] Jaquette, p. 21.

[152] Jaquette, p. 154.

[153] Jaquette, p. 11.

[154] Jaquette, p. 62.

[155] Jaquette, p. 57.

[154] John R. Brumgardt, Ed., *Civil War Nurse, The Diary and Letters of Hannah Ropes,* The University of Tennessee, Knoxville, 1980, p. 57

[157] Jaquette, p. 20-21.

[158] Wiley, p. 125.

[159] Jaquette, p. 58

[160] Rutkow, p. 25

[161] Civil War Medicine Page, http://www.civilwarhome.com/civilwarmedicine.htm, Source: The Civil War Society's "Encyclopedia of the Civil War," June 30, 2009.

[162] Bollet, p. 166-178.

[163] Bollet, p. 38-55 and 165-6.

[164] Bollet, p. 162.

[165] Freemon, p. 48.

[166] Bollet, p. 93.

[167] Civil War Medicine Page, http://www.civilwarhome.com/civilwarmedicine.htm, Source: The Civil War Society's "Encyclopedia of the Civil War," June 30, 2009.

[168] Civil War Medicine Page, http://www.civilwarhome.com/civilwarmedicineintro.htm Article by Edward L. Musnson, M.D. Major, Medical Department, United States Army, June 30, 2009.

[169] Paul Fatout, *Letters of a Civil War Surgeon,* Purdue University Studies, (West Lafayette, 1961) p. 63

[170] Jaquette, p. 67.

[171] Jaquette, p. 86-7.

[172] Freemon, p. 75.

[173] National Park Service, "Voices of Battle," http://www.nps.gov/archive/gett/getttour/sidebar/letterman.htm, May 31, 2010.

[174] Jaquette, p. 24.

[175] Jane McConnell, p. 64-75.

[176] Jaquette, p. vi.

[177] Oates, p. 15.

[178] Jaquette, p. 44.

[179] Jaquette, p. 41.

[180] Jaquette, p. 44-5.

[181] Jaquette, p. 40-1

[182] Robert Dale Owen, J. McKaye, Saml.. G. Howe, Commissioners, Source: "Official Records of the War of the Rebellion", http://www.civilwarhome.com/commissionreport.htm, June 23, 2009.

[183] Jaquette, p. 31.

[184] Jaquette, p. 44.

[185] Jaquette, p. 51.

[186] Jaquette, p. 46.

[187] Jaquette, p. 51.

[188] Reid Mitchell, *Civil War Soldiers*, Viking Adult, (New York, 1988), p. 185.

[189] Jaquette, p. 21.

[190] Bollet, p. 243.

[191] Mitchell, 67-88.

[192] Jaquette, p.59

[193] http://www.civilwarhome.com/camplife.htm, Source: The Civil War Society's "Encyclopedia of the Civil War," February 21, 2010.

[194] Wiley, p. 124-8.

[195] Jaquette, p. 83

[196] "The Medical and Surgical History of the War of the Rebellion. (1861-65.) Part III, Volume II, Chapter XIV.--The Medical Staff and Materia Chirugic.

[197] Jaquette, p. 129 & 130.

[198] Bollet, p. 271.

[199] The Civil War Society's "Encyclopedia of the Civil War" http://www.civilwarhome.com/civilwarmedicine.htm, February 21, 2010.

[200] Wiley, p. 133-6.

[201] Bollet, p. 291.

[202] OSU Department of History, eHistory at The Ohio State University, February 21, 2010.

[203] Rutkow, p. 125.

[204] Freemon, p. 202.

[205] Bollet, p. 49-50.

[206] Bollet, p. 291.

[207] Joseph Jacobs, Pharmacist, Atlanta, Georgia, "Some Of The Drug Conditions During The War Between The States, 1861-5" A Paper read before a meeting of the American Pharmaceutical Association held in Baltimore, Maryland, in August, 1898

[138] Ibid

[209] Bollet, p. 352.

[210] Joseph Jacob paper.

211 John S. Salmon, Staff Historian Virginia Department of Historic Resources http://www.nps.gov/history/NR/travel/journey/civilwar.htm, March 6, 2010

212 Fatout, p. 84 and 90

213 Wayne Motts, Audio Tour, Gettysburg Field Guide, Travel Brains, Inc. 2008.

214 Jaquette, p. 51.

215 "Some of the Wonders of Modern Surgery," *The Atlantic Monthly*, vol. 21, no. 125, (March, 1868): p. 26.

216 Straubing, p. 19.

217 Jaquette, p. 120

218 Jaquette, p. 90.

219 Jaquette, p. 92.

220 National Park Service, Fredericksburg & Spotsylvania County Memorial Battlefields, http://www.nps.gov/frsp/wildspot.htm May 26, 2010.

221 Jaquette, p. 93.

222 Jaquette, p. 120.

223 Jaquette, p. 148-50.

224 Ulysses S. Grant, *Memoirs and Selected Letters,* The Library of America, (New York, 1990), p. 546-549.

225 Jaquette, p. 131.

226 Jaquette, p. 82.

227 Jaquette, p. 90.

228 Jaquette, p. 95-6.

229 Edward L. Musnson, M.D. Major, Medical Department, United States Army, http://www.civilwarhome.com/armysurgeon.htm   June 30, 2009.

230 National Park Service Battle Summary, http://www.nps.gov/history/hps/abpp/battles/va048.htm June 23, 2009.

231 Jaquette, p. 109.

232 Grant, p. 583-4.

233 Jaquette, p. 98-9.

234 Jaquette, p. 99.

235 Jaquette, p. 101-02.

236 Jaquette p. 117.

237 Jaquette, p. 137.

238 Jaquette, p. 124-5.

239 Jaquette, p. 144.

240 Jaquette, p. 179.

241 Jaquette, p. 179.

242 H. E. Brown, The Medical Department of the United States Army from 1775 to 1873, Washington, Surgeon General's Office, 1873, p. 245.

243 Bollet, p. 423.

244 http://faculty.uml.edu/awalters/43.233/diseasehand6b.doc, June 24, 2009.

[245] Mary R. Dearing, *Veterans in Politics,* Louisiana State University Press, (Baton Rouge, 1952), p. 50.

[246] Jaquette, p.182

[247] Dearing, p. 51-4.

[248] Dearing, p. 72.

[249] Stuart Charles McConnell, *Glorious contentment: the Grand Army of the Republic,* (University of North Carolina Press, 1992,) p. 127.

[250] Jane McConnell, p. 149.

[251] Jaquette, p. 185

[252] Shelby Foote, Performance in Episode One of the Ken Burns' film *The Civil War,* 1983

[253] Shelby Foote, Episode One of the Ken Burns' film *The Civil War,* 1983

[254] Stuart McConnell, 22.

[255] Grant, p. 511.

[256] Stuart McConnell, p. 168-71.

[257] Joyce Appleby, *Inheriting the Revolution: the First Generation of Americans,* The Belknap Press, 2000, p. 231.

[258] Appleby, "New Cultural Heroes," 163–88, esp. 166; Robert H. Wiebe, *The Opening of American Society: From the Adoption of the Constitution to the Eve of Disunion* (New York: Knopf, 1984).

[259] Brockett and Vaughan, p. 68.

[260] Florence Nightingale, *Notes on Nursing,* Dover Publications, 1969, p 133.

[261] Nightingale, p. 135.

[262] Oates, p. 376.

[263] Oates, p. 376.

[264] Brockett and Vaughan, p.21

[265] Brockett and Vaughan, p. 285-6.

[266] Schultz, p. 233-4.

[241] Jaquette, p. xii.

[268] Schultz, p. 147.

[269] Brockett and Vaughan, p. 57.

[270] Jaquette, p. 87

[271] Jaquette, p. xii.

[272] Jaquette, p. 72.

[273] Jaquette, p. 76.

[274] Jaquette, p. 75-6.

[275] Jane McConnell, p. 175-6.

[276] Located in Salem, New Jersey.

[277] Patricia L. Faust, Editor, "Historical Times Illustrated Encyclopedia of the Civil War" and Mark M. Boatner III "The Civil War Dictionary," Definitions of Civil War Terms, http://www.civilwarhome.com/terms.htm, May 27, 2010

[278] Jaquette, p. 156.

[279] Eric Foner and Olivia Mahoney, *America's Reconstruction: People and Politics After the Civil War,* http://www.digitalhistory.uh.edu/reconstruction/credits.html, May 11, 2010.

[280] Jaquette, p. 185.

[281] Jaquette, p. 213

[282] Jaquette, p. 189-90.

[283] Jaquette, p. 194.

[284] *American Experience, Reconstruction the Second Civil War,* http://www.pbs.org/wgbh/amex/reconstruction/40acres/ps_so15.html, June 30, 2009.

[285] American Experience, Reconstruction the Second Civil War, http://www.pbs.org/wgbh/amex/reconstruction/states/sf_timeline.html, July 12, 2010.

[286] Jaquette, p. 192.

[287] Jaquette, p. 186.

[288] Jaquette, p. 213.

[289] Jaquette, p. 213.

[290] Jaquette, p. 218-21.

[291] Jaquette, p. 216.

[292] Jaquette, p. 223.

[293] Jaquette, p. 212.

[294] Jaquette, p. 217.

[295] Jaquette, p. 265.

[296] Meade, p. 292-3.

[297] Mitchell, p. 204.

[298] Mitchell, p.207-8.

[299] Stuart McConnell, p. 168-173.

[300] Mitchell, p. 208.

[301] Stuart McConnell, p. 174.

[302] Jaquette, p. 241.

[303] Jaquette, p. 239.

[304] Jaquette, p. 287-8.

[305] Maritime Exchange for the Delaware River and Bay, http://www.maritimedelriv.com/our_history.htm, May 11, 2010

[306] http://www.bankcrash.nl/english/historythelongdepression.php, May 11, 2010.

[307] Philadelphia Society for Organizing Charity, Volume: 1, Philadelphia, Pa. Internet Archive, American Libraries, http://www.archive.org/details/papersofphiladel01phil, May 10, 2010

[308] Jane McConnell, p. 176-7.

[309] Edward T. James, Janet Wilson James, Paul S. Boyer, *Notable American women, 1607-1950: a biographical dictionary, Volume 2,* Radcliffe College, (Cambridge, 1971,) p. 128-9.

[310] The Cornelia Hancock Auxiliary #10, http://www.lyoncamp.org/cornelia.htm, May 10, 2010

[311] Adams, p. 71-2.

[312] Sophronia E. Bucklin, Hospital and Camp, John E. Potter and Company, (Philadelphia, 1869), 248.

[313] Jaquette, p. 67.

[306] Jaquette, p. 247

[315] Jaquette, p. 147.

[316] Jaquette, p. 148

[317] Civil War Armies Page, Source: "Civil War Dictionary" By Mark M. Boatner III and "The Historical Times Encyclopedia of the Civil War" edited by Patricia L. Faust http://www.civilwarhome.com/armyorganization.htm, April 1, 2010